An Italian Affair

Italian Cooking So Simple... It's Scandalous

An Italian Affair

Shelley Sikora

7633 Via Del Reposo
Scottsdale, Arizona 85258,
USA.

Cover design by Patrick Henry Creative Promotions, Houston, TX
Book design by CB Studios, Phoenix, AZ

Library of Congress Cataloguing-in-Publication Data

Sikora, Shelley

      An Italian Affair™/Shelley Sikora
      p. cm.
      ISBN 0-9724749-0-0 (pbk.)
      1. Cooking 2. Italian 1. Sikora, Shelley, In The Mood To Cook, Inc.
      LCCD 2001118222

™ 76/369398

First Edition, September 2002

*Dedicated with love to my mother
Gerloma "May" Pino-Acquaro.
Gifted chef, baker and loving Matriarch of our family.*

ACKNOWLEDGEMENTS

This book is a celebration of Sicilian cooking that was
put together through the Divine intervention of our Creator.

My friend and editor, Hallie Harron, provided the
creative input, encouragement and direction that only a
true visionary could do. My friends
who are my support staff, especially Kevin McAullife,
Ron and Becky Walton, Ron and Bobbi Newman, and so many
others who helped encourage and support this process.

Michael Shapiro, teacher and friend who encourages
creativity, meditation and a willingness to go within.

To all my family for their recipes, their love, their years of conversation,
memories and laughter. My brother, Father Phil for his support throughout
all the years, along with his baking of all the cookie recipes and many
scholarly days of editing. My daughter Brooke for being the lovely,
caring and supportive person that she is.

And most importantly, my loving soulmate, partner and husband,
Bob Sikora, the Quintessential mastermind with an eye for
photography, and ear for music, a smell for a great project
and the loving touch of a husband.

I love and sincerely "Thank You" all.

Contents

CHAPTER 1   Family Platters to Share

CHAPTER 2   Friends Foods to Entertain With

CHAPTER 3   **Sundays and Special Occasions**
                  Simply Special Dishes

CHAPTER 4   **Traditions, Romance and Weddings**
                  Delicious Party Foods

CHAPTER 8 Bread, Wine, Cheese, Olives and Herbs
Simple Foods to Savor

CHAPTER 9 Pizza Thick & Thin, Rolled and Folded

Preface

'An Italian Affair' celebrates the reunion of food and family. This book gathers generations of recipes from my family's historical Sicilian roots in the farmlands of Partenico and Palermo, Sicily. Traditions, customs and food from these regions demonstrate the need to gather together around the kitchen table for conversation and create the genuine warm feelings that come from eating food in a family environment.

Sicilian home cooking from my family's kitchen is not very fancy or trendy, but it is truly great food! This cookbook is lively, simple and as down-to-earth as the roots it came from. There are lots of tips and shortcuts to provide maximum flavor with minimum time, the Sicilian way.

About the Author

SHELLEY 'ACQUARO' SIKORA, daughter of Philip and May Acquaro is a second generation Sicilian-American born in Detroit, Michigan.

Her mom, May, whose family was originally from Partenico, Sicily, is an outstanding professional cook and baker who specializes in desserts and wedding cakes. Shelley was fortunate enough to learn how to cook from May. To this day, Shelley and her brother, Father Phil, still bake with Mom every week.

Shelley spent 15 years in the broadcasting and advertising business that took her from Detroit to Dallas, Denver and Phoenix. She then joined her husband in the restaurant business in 1985 where she was able to develop her passion for cooking. She is a member of the International Association of Culinary Professionals, and has studied under many culinary chefs.

Shelley and her husband, Bob, owned a large chain of 24 restaurants that reached from the United States to Australia. Today they own and operate one of those restaurants in Phoenix. They have one daughter, Brooke, who lives in Washington, D.C. who, of course, loves to cook. Currently the Sikora's reside in Scottsdale, Arizona with their two canine kids, Ruby and Yogi.

CHAPTER 1

FAMILY-PLATTERS TO SHARE

The history of Sicily is the history of close-knit families. In the early 1900's, our families, named Amato, Pino and Acquaro, left Partenico, Sicily, to seek a new life in Detroit, Michigan. Along with great hopes, courage, and humor our families brought their heritage of hearty, flavorful and welcoming food.

Sicilian cooking is intriguingly simple. Thank goodness! Large family gatherings are normal in our household. We're not the once a year holiday party kind of group. Instead we meet regularly to happily enjoy lots of simply prepared plates. Lots of conversation, lots of sampling, lots of people. We're Sicilian!

You'll find that most of the recipes are easy, fairly hearty, and really fun to put together either on your own or with help from the family. For any given meal, select as many dishes as you wish. We usually choose quite a few to make on any given occasion, allowing for lots of variety and options.

"Everything you see around me I owe to spaghetti."— *My feelings and those of Sophia Loren*

ANTIPASTI-"Before the meal" dishes. Beware! These recipes are so tempting and seductive that just a handful can make up a whole dinner!

BRUSCHETTA
These slices of toasted bread were used in Italy as a way of tasting the freshly pressed olive oil. Hot grilled bread is dipped in oil and rubbed with garlic. It is often topped with tomatoes.

> 1 loaf of Italian bread or French baguette, cut into
>   1-inch slices
> 3-4 large ripe tomatoes, chopped
> 3 Tbs. fresh basil, chopped
> 1/3 cup extra-virgin olive oil
> 3 to 4 garlic cloves, peeled and diced
> Freshly grated Parmesan cheese (optional)

Toast or grill bread until golden brown on both sides. In a small bowl, mix together tomatoes, basil, oil and garlic. Spoon mixture onto toast. Sprinkle with cheese, if desired.
Serve warm.

Serves 8-10

PIPING HOT BREAD AND GREAT OIL

There's nothing like a hot, fresh loaf of Italian bread. Whether you choose to make the bread (see our bread recipe, pg. 136), or opt for a local Italian bakery, this super simple recipe can easily turn into dinner.

> 1 loaf fresh hard-crusted Italian bread
> Best quality extra-virgin olive oil
> Salt and pepper to taste.

If your bread is still oven-fresh 'hot', pour on some of the olive oil, a pinch of salt and pepper, and eat it!

If the loaf of bread is fresh, but not hot, preheat oven to 350 degrees. Cut the loaf in half lengthwise and place it crust side down on a sheet of tin foil. Drizzle it with a generous amount of olive oil. Wrap the loaf in foil, leaving a small exposed space to prevent bread from steaming. Bake for 10-15 minutes or until very hot. For a crispier crust, open foil packet, turn the bread over and brown the crust for a few minutes.

Serves 3-4

FRESH MOZZARELLA AND TOMATO SALAD

Make this antipasto a few hours and store it in the refrigerator. Just remember to bring it to room temperature before serving.

> 4 large ripe tomatoes, cut in 1/2-inch slices
> 6-8 oz. fresh Mozzarella cheese, cut in 1/2-inch slices
> 4 Tbs. extra-virgin olive oil
> 3 Tbs. Balsamic vinegar
> 4 Tbs. fresh basil, chopped
> Salt and pepper to taste

Alternate tomato and cheese slices on a large serving platter. Drizzle the oil and vinegar over the top. Sprinkle with basil, salt and pepper. Cover and refrigerate.

Serves 6

ONE CLASSIC ANTIPASTO

'Before the pasta,' or antipasto, can include vegetables, fish, cured meats and seasonal fruit. Here's our family version to wake up your appetite. At our house, we love to serve it with fresh Italian bread and a dish of olive oil.

> 2 small zucchini, thinly sliced
> 1 small yellow squash, thinly sliced
> 1 red pepper, cut in thin strips
> 4 Tbs. extra-virgin olive oil
> 10 thin slices of Genoa salami
> 6 paper-thin slices of prosciutto
> 1 small jar of marinated mushrooms
> 1 small jar of hot yellow peppers
> 6 thin slices of provolone cheese
> 1 lb. of black Italian or Greek olives
> Salt and pepper to taste
> Fresh Italian parsley sprigs

Heat oven to broil. Place all vegetables in a large bowl and toss with olive oil. Place on a cookie sheet. Place cookie sheet close to the heat source and broil vegetables on both sides until light brown or tender to touch. Remove from broiler and set aside. On a large platter, arrange all ingredients except the seasonings in a colorful pattern. Sprinkle with salt and pepper and top with sprigs of parsley.

Serves 6

ROASTED GARLIC

Ancient Romans and definitely Sicilians have used garlic to cure all ills. There is no better tasting remedy to share with your family any time of year.

> 1 extra large garlic bulb
> 1 Tbs. extra-virgin olive oil
> Salt and pepper to taste

Preheat oven to 350 degrees. Peel the first papery skin of the garlic, leaving the bulb whole. Place it upright on a sheet of aluminum foil. Drizzle with olive oil and season with salt and pepper. Tightly seal the foil. Bake for 45 minutes or until very soft when pressed. Alternatively if you have a special garlic roasting dish, put the bulb in the dish, season, and bake as directed. Serve either in its whole form or squeeze the cloves from the bulb and place in a small dish. Serve the warm garlic on fresh slices of Italian bread.

Serves 2

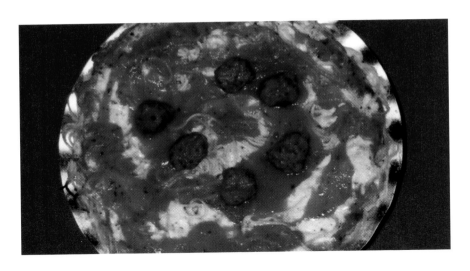

SPAGHETTI PIE

This household favorite takes only 30 minutes to assemble and can be done one day in advance. Bake it just before serving.

> 1 lb. spaghetti
> 1 Tbs. olive oil
> 1/3 cup Parmesan cheese, grated
> 2 eggs, beaten
> 1 Tbs. dried basil
> 1 Tbs. dried oregano
> 1/2 tsp. each salt and pepper
> 1 3/4 cups ricotta cheese
> 3 cups spaghetti sauce (see sauce recipe, pg. 125)
> 2 cups mozzarella cheese, shredded

Preheat oven to 350 degrees. Cook spaghetti in 1 gallon boiling water to which you've added 1 Tbs. oil. When pasta is half cooked, but still very firm, drain it and rinse with cold water to stop further cooking. Set aside.

In a large bowl, thoroughly mix together all of the ingredients except the pasta, sauce and mozzarella cheese. Then blend in the spaghetti thoroughly. Lightly oil a large, round deep-dish pie pan. Spoon in 1/3 of the spaghetti mixture and press to form a pasta crust on sides and bottom of the pie pan. Then spoon in remaining spaghetti mixture. Top with 1 cup of the sauce. Cover with foil and bake for 45 minutes, or until pie is hot and bubbly. Remove and let pie rest for 10 minutes before serving. Serve along with remaining sauce on warm plates or serve at the table on a large warm platter.

Serves 8

BAKED ZITI

Need another wonderful alternative to lasagne? Here's one of my personal favorites.

> 1 15 oz. container part-skim ricotta cheese
> 2 eggs, beaten
> 1/3 cup Parmesan cheese, grated
> 1 1/2 lbs. ziti pasta, cooked and drained
> About 1 cup per serving Spaghetti Sauce
> (see traditional sauce recipe, pg. 125)
> 1 cup Mozzarella cheese, shredded

Preheat oven to 350 degrees. In large bowl, combine ricotta cheese, eggs and Parmesan cheese. Set aside. In another large bowl, thoroughly combine hot pasta and marinara sauce.
In a lightly oiled 13 x 9-inch baking dish, spoon in 1/2 of the pasta mixture. Top with ricotta mixture, then top with remaining ziti. Sprinkle with mozzarella cheese. Cover with foil or a tight cover. Bake 30 minutes or until heated through. Remove foil and bake an additional 5 minutes or until lightly browned.

Serves 12

CHICKEN PARMESAN

You'll have plenty of sauce left with this recipe. Make your favorite pasta, toss it with the sauce and serve it alongside the chicken. Now that's Italian!

> 3 eggs, lightly beaten
> 2 cups fresh bread crumbs
> 8 boneless, skinless chicken breast halves, pounded thin
> 1/4 cup vegetable oil
> About 8 cups spaghetti sauce (see sauce recipe pg. 125)
> 2 cups Mozzarella cheese, shredded
> 1/2 cup Parmesan cheese, grated (optional)
> 1 tsp. dried oregano
> 1/2 tsp. salt
> 1 tsp. ground dried bay leaves

Preheat oven to 375°. Place eggs in a shallow bowl and spread breadcrumbs onto a large plate. Dip chicken first in eggs, then press thoroughly into the crumbs. In a large skillet, heat oil over medium high. Brown chicken in batches, then place them on a paper-toweled lined baking sheet. Pour 1 1/2 cups spaghetti sauce into a 13x9-inch baking dish. Place chicken over sauce, then top with remaining sauce. Sprinkle with oregano and salt, then top with mozzarella and Parmesan cheese. Cover with foil and bake 30 minutes or until heated through and the cheese is melted. Remove cover and bake an additional 5 minutes.

Serves 8

BREADED PORTERHOUSE 'BISTECCA'

I have yet to find a better way to serve steaks on the grill. This summer favorite is always tender and moist and guaranteed to please all hearty appetites.

4 large ripe tomatoes, diced
1/2 cup water
8 garlic cloves, minced
1/2 tsp. each garlic salt and black pepper
1 Tbs. dried basil
1 Tbs. dried oregano
3/4 cup olive oil
6 1-inch thick porterhouse steaks
4 cups Italian breadcrumbs

In a medium bowl, stir together the tomatoes, water, garlic, garlic salt, pepper, basil, oregano and 1/4 cup olive oil. Stir and mash tomatoes down to extract their juice and set aside. Heat a grill to medium.

Pour remaining olive oil onto a flat platter. Place breadcrumbs on a large flat plate. Wipe the steaks with a paper towel to remove excess moisture then dip each side in oil. Press each side firmly into the crumbs to cover the meat completely.

Grill the steaks until juices begin to accumulate on the surface. Turn the meat and generously baste with the tomato mixture. Continue cooking to desired doneness. Serve topped with remaining basting sauce.

Serves 6

SICILIAN POT ROAST

When I was growing up, my working mom would prepare pot roast during the week, rather than on Sundays like so many other Sicilian households. We would always invite lots of family and friends over on these nights as there was always plenty of welcome and pot roast to go around. When you make this don't forget to include a large loaf of fresh Italian bread.

> 2 Tbs. fennel seed, crushed
> 2 Tbs. dried parsley, crushed
> 4 tsps. dried Italian seasoning, crushed
> 1/2 tsp. garlic salt
> 1 tsp. pepper
> 1 Tbs. olive oil
> 1 beef eye of round, about 3 1/2-4 lbs.
> 3/4 cup water
> 6 carrots, quartered
> 1 1/2 lbs. small potatoes, peeled
> 3 celery stalks, chopped into 2-inch pieces
> 2 garlic cloves, minced
> 1 medium onion, finely chopped
> 1/4 cup flour

Heat oven to 325 degrees. In a small bowl, mix together fennel seed, parsley, Italian seasoning, garlic salt, and pepper. Set aside.

In a large pot, heat the oil over medium heat. Rub seasoning mixture on both sides of meat. Brown all sides well in oil. Carefully drain fat from pot. Pour in 3/4 cup water. Roast the meat, uncovered, 1 1/2 to 2 hours or until meat is cooked but not quite tender. Arrange vegetables and garlic around the meat, cover with foil, and roast an additional 50 minutes to one hour or until vegetables and meat are tender. Add a little water to the pan if all juices evaporate during roasting. Remove and let meat stand for 15 minutes, covered. Transfer vegetables to a serving dish and cover.

Skim fat from the pan juices and strain, if desired. Add water as needed to make 1 1/2 cups. In a small bowl, mix together the flour and 1/2 cup water. Bring pan juices to a rapid boil over medium heat. Then gradually whisk flour mixture into gravy. Whisk until smooth. Cook for 1 more minute. Remove from heat and serve with pot roast. Serve the carved roast on a warm platter, surrounded by vegetables and sauce.

Serves 8

SWEET POTATO GNOCCHI

Here's our version of an Italian potato dumpling. Our Sicilian version is made with sweet potatoes, not the usual Idaho spuds. These freeze beautifully in sealed zip lock bags so make them ahead for last minute, impromptu parties.

> 1 1/2 lbs. sweet potatoes, peeled and quartered
> 1 cup part-skim ricotta cheese
> 1/2 tsp. salt
> 3/4 tsp. nutmeg
> 2 cups all-purpose flour
> Extra-virgin olive oil
> Freshly ground pepper
> Parmesan cheese, grated
> 2 Tbs. Italian parsley, chopped

In a large saucepan cook sweet potatoes in boiling, salted water, covered, for 25 to 30 minutes or until tender. Drain in a colander and return them to the same pot. In order to remove any excess moisture, mash potatoes over low heat with a potato masher until smooth. Transfer mixture to a large bowl. Stir in ricotta cheese, salt, nutmeg, and 1 1/2 cups of the flour.

On a well-floured surface, knead in the remaining 1/2-cup flour, kneading for 2 to 3 minutes or until dough forms a soft ball. Divide into 8 pieces. With well-floured hands, roll each piece of dough into a 12-inch log, about 1 inch around. Cut logs crosswise into 1-inch pieces. With a floured finger, make a dimple in the center of each one.

In a large pot of boiling salted water, cook several gnocchi at a time, 3 to 4 minutes or until they rise to the surface. Do not overcook! Carefully remove with a slotted spoon to a paper towel-lined tray to drain. Lightly cover to keep warm while cooking remaining gnocchi.

Place gnocchi on a warm serving platter. Drizzle gnocchi with olive oil to lightly coat. Dust top with freshly ground pepper and cheese. Sprinkle the gnocchi with parsley and serve.

Makes 16 side dish servings or about 95 gnocchi

STRACIATELLA Italian Egg Drop Soup

Egg drop soup is usually associated with Chinese cooking. This soup, however, is also very popular in Sicily. My mom used to serve it every Sunday, especially if anyone in the family was under the weather. It's a tasty remedy, but delicious anytime.

    10 cups homemade or canned chicken broth
    4 eggs
    6 Tbs. Parmesan cheese
    1 cup Italian parsley, chopped
    Salt and pepper to taste

In a large 4-quart soup pot, bring broth to a boil over moderate heat. In a small bowl, beat together the eggs, cheese and parsley. Reduce the heat to low and drizzle eggs into stock, gently stirring. Simmer, stirring, just until eggs are set. Season with salt and pepper and serve hot.

Serves 8

CHICKEN CACCIATORE

In Sicily, one pot casserole-style cooking is very popular. If stove top space is at a premium, just pop the pan in a 350 degree oven for 1 1/2 hours. Remember to use young spring chicks for this. The older birds are just too tough.

> 2 - 3 lb. chickens, each cut into 6-8 pieces
> 3/4 cup flour, seasoned with salt and pepper
> 1/2 cup olive oil
> 4 garlic cloves, minced
> 1 14.5 oz. can stewed tomatoes
> 1 15 oz. can tomato sauce
> 2 large potatoes, cut in 2-inch wedges
> 2 stalks of celery, cut in 2 -inch pieces
> 2 medium onions, chopped
> 1/2 large red bell pepper, chopped
> 4 tsp. each dried oregano and parsley
> 6 fresh basil leaves or 1 1/2 tsp. dried
> 1/4 cup white wine
> 1 cup red wine vinegar
> 1/4 cup sugar
> Fresh basil leaves for garnish

Dredge chicken in seasoned flour. Heat oil in a large skillet over medium heat and brown chicken in batches on both sides, about 5 minutes on each side. Transfer chicken to a paper towel lined baking sheet to remove excess oil. Set aside. Add garlic to skillet and sauté over medium heat for 1 minute. Add potatoes, celery, onions, pepper, stewed tomatoes and tomato sauce and cook until potatoes are light brown. Add herbs and then, stirring constantly, slowly add wine. Return the chicken to the pan. Heat sauce to boiling, add vinegar and sugar, then reduce the heat to low. Cover skillet and cook for about 45 minutes or until chicken is tender. Transfer to a large platter and serve topped with fresh basil sprigs.

Serves 6-8

SHRIMP SICILIANO

Not everyone loves fish, but almost everyone adores our shrimp platters served on a bed of tomatoes. Make sure to assemble all the ingredients before cooking.

> 4 Tbs. olive oil
> 5-6 garlic cloves, minced
> 2 lbs. large (16-20 count) shrimp, shelled and de-veined
> 3-4 medium size fresh Roma tomatoes, diced
> 1 stalk celery, diced
> 1/2 cup tomato sauce
> 1 tsp. each dried oregano and basil
> 3/4 cup dry white wine
> Salt and pepper to taste
> 1/2 cup Parmesan cheese, grated
> Fresh Italian parsley sprig

In a large skillet, heat 2 tablespoons olive oil over medium heat. Sauté garlic until golden brown. Add all remaining ingredients except cheese and parsley, including remaining oil, and sauté the shrimp until pink and firm about 10-12 minutes. Sprinkle with Parmesan and serve immediately, topped with a sprig of Italian parsley.

Serves 4-6

FAMILY STYLE DESSERTS

All of the following recipes have been served at our family gatherings for years. For every special holiday, each family is normally assigned a dessert. Here are some of our favorites.

CAPPUCCINO GRANITA

Granita is an Italian ice, a granular frozen dessert, that requires no ice cream maker to prepare. This Sicilian classic starts with double-strength, dark roast Italian brewed coffee that gives an intense flavor when it is frozen. Granitas will keep for 1 month.

> 1/2 cup freshly ground dark Italian roast coffee beans
> 1 3/4 cups water
> 1/3 cup each sugar and water
> 1 tsp. vanilla extract
> 1/4 tsp. ground cinnamon
> 1/2 cup 1% low-fat milk
> Mint sprigs (optional)

Make coffee with beans and water. Set aside to cool. In a small saucepan, bring sugar and 1/3 cup water to a boil. Cook one minute or until sugar dissolves. Stir in vanilla and cinnamon. Remove from heat, and stir in brewed coffee and milk. Cool mixture completely and pour into an 8-inch square baking dish. Cover and freeze at least 8 hours or until firm. Remove dish from freezer and scrape with a fork until fluffy. Spoon into a freezer-safe container. If desired, serve topped with fresh mint sprigs.

Serves 6, about 2/3 cup each

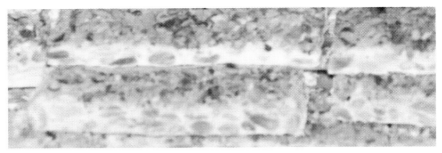

TORRONE

Every year, as soon as almonds are harvested, Sicilian house-holds set about making fresh Torrone. In our house, it's a year long treat. We store it in an airtight jar.

> 2 lbs. shelled whole almonds
> 2 cups shelled whole pistachio nuts
> 5 cups white sugar
> 2 cups honey
> 2 cups hulled sesame seeds
> Drop of almond extract
> Wafer Sheets (found at Italian specialty stores)

Generously spray a 12"x 18" baking dish with cooking spray. Heat oven to 350 degrees. Place the nuts on a baking sheet and toast for 5 minutes or until very warm to the touch. Let cool.

In a large heavy saucepan, carefully cook the sugar until it melts, then stir in the honey. Over low heat, add the nuts, sesame seeds, and almond extract. Stir until the honey dissolves. Cook until a teaspoon of the mixture hardens when dropped into a small cup of water. Line a mold or rectangular baking pan with the thin sheets of unleavened wafer. Pour in the mixture making an even layer, top with another wafer, cover with a wooden board and weight the board down. When the torrone hardens and looks like a sheet of glass, overturn pan onto on a hard surface and cut into rectangles. Serve or wrap candy squares in parchment and store in an airtight container.

Makes about 30 small squares

ITALIAN RUM CAKE

We did it our way! This popular family cake has a twist to streamline the process. As a working mom, my mother didn't have the time to prepare all the custards and cakes from scratch. She was however a real kitchen genius! No one ever knew the difference. The flavor was and still is sublime!

> 4 eggs
> 1/2 cup cold water
> 1/2 cup vegetable oil
> 1/2 cup light rum
> 1 package yellow cake mix
> 1 package vanilla instant pudding

Glaze:

> 1/4 lb. butter, room temperature
> 1/2 cup water
> 1 cup powdered sugar
> 1/2 cup light rum
> 1 cup walnuts, chopped

Preheat oven to 325 degrees. Grease and flour a tube or Bundt cake pan. In a large mixing bowl, beat the eggs. Add the water, oil and rum. Slowly beat in the cake and pudding mix. Pour into prepared pan and bake according to the cake mix directions. When cake is done, remove from oven and cool.
For glaze, beat together the butter, water, sugar and rum, until it is smooth. Drizzle glaze over cake, sprinkle with the nuts and refrigerate until ready to serve.

Serves 8-10

TORTA FRUTTA

Everyone loves cousin Francie's one-step pound cake. Serve a slice of this treat with fresh berries or any seasonal fruit, frozen yogurt or a scoop of Italian ice.

> 1 cup butter, room temperature
> 2 cups granulated sugar
> 2 1/4 cups all-purpose flour
> 1/2 tsp. baking soda
> 1/2 tsp. salt
> 1 8 oz. container pineapple or orange yogurt
> 3 eggs, lightly beaten
> 1 tsp. grated lemon or orange zest
> 1 tsp. vanilla
> 1/2 cup confectioner's sugar
> 2 Tbs. lemon juice
> Fresh mint leaves and/or fresh fruit, berries, Italian ice

Preheat oven to 325 degrees. Grease and flour a Bundt or tube pan. In a large mixing bowl, beat together butter, sugar, flour, baking soda, salt, yogurt, eggs, zest, and vanilla at low speed, then increase speed until well blended, about 10 minutes. Pour into pan. Bake for 50-60 minutes. Remove to a cookie or cooling rack. While cake is cooling, whisk together powdered sugar and lemon juice and blend until smooth. Drizzle over cooled cake. Top each slice with a mint leaf and or a slice of fresh fruit, berries or Italian ice.

Serves 16

RASPBERRY DOLCI DI CREMA

This is a rich raspberry cream in a crunchy cookie shell that cousin Joe and Anthony brought to many family dinners. Make it! It's exceptionally delicious.

For cookie crust:
>   1 1/2 cups all-purpose flour
>   1/2 cup butter, at room temperature
>   1/3 cup sugar
>   1 egg white

For filling:
>   1/4 cup sugar
>   3 Tbs. all-purpose flour
>   1 envelope unflavored gelatin
>   1/4 tsp. salt
>   2 eggs plus 1 yolk
>   1 1/2 cups milk
>   1 Tbs. amaretto or 1/2 tsp. almond extract
>   1/2 cup whipping cream
>   1/2 pint fresh raspberries, washed
>
>   1/2 cup raspberry jam

Preheat oven to 350 degrees. In a medium bowl, stir together flour, butter and sugar. Turn out onto a floured surface and gently knead until mixture holds together. Pat into the bottom and sides of a 10-inch tart or springform pan with removable bottom. Bake 20 minutes or until golden brown.

In a small cup, beat the egg white with a fork. Brush onto hot cookie crust. Cool crust in pan on wire rack, then remove crust from pan.

In a heavy, 2-quart saucepan, mix sugar, flour, gelatin and salt. In a medium bowl, beat eggs, yolk and milk with a fork until blended. Stir into sugar mixture. Cook over medium-low heat, stirring constantly, until gelatin is completely dissolved and mixture thickens enough to coat the back of a spoon, about 15 minutes. Don't let the custard boil. Remove from heat and stir in almond liqueur or extract. Chill 1 hour, or until mixture mounds slightly. In a small bowl, beat whipping cream until soft peaks form. Fold into chilled custard. Spoon custard into pastry shell. In a small saucepan, melt the jam and marble it through the custard with a knife. Arrange fresh raspberries on top. Refrigerate 1 hour, or until custard is set.

Serves 8-10

CHAPTER 2

FRIENDS-FOODS TO ENTERTAIN WITH

My life seems to have begun on the end of a fork. As a result, friends always seem to end up in our kitchen. Inevitably, conversations start and end with food. Try out some of these "comfort food for friends" recipes any time simply good fare without fuss is called for. They are all user-friendly, unfussy dishes to share with your dearest friends.

CROSTINI DI CAPONATA

This not so common appetizer is easy to prepare. All you need are small slices of crusty bread and a handful of fresh ingredients for the top. The caponata can be made one or two days in advance. It's best served at room temperature.

Caponata:
     1 Tbs. extra-virgin olive oil
     1 medium eggplant,diced
     1 medium sweet onion (Vidalia if possible), chopped
     1/2 small red bell pepper, diced
     1/2 small yellow bell pepper, diced
     1 garlic clove, minced
     1 Tbs. brown sugar
     2 Tbs. lemon juice
     1/2 tsp. garlic salt
     1/2 cup golden raisins
     2 Tbs. capers
     1 Tbs. toasted pine nuts
     3 Tbs. fresh basil, chopped

Crostini:
     4 garlic cloves, minced
     2/3 cup olive oil
     1 long French baguette , cut 24 diagonal 1/2 inch slices

     Parmesan Cheese, optional

In a large skillet, heat oil over medium heat. Add eggplant, onion, peppers and minced garlic. Saute for 5 minutes. Stir in sugar, lemon juice and garlic salt. Cook, stirring, for 1 minute. Add raisins, capers and pine nuts, and remove from heat. Transfer mixture to a bowl and fold in basil. Set aside or refrigerate.

To serve:

Heat oven to 375 degrees. In a small bowl, mix together garlic and oil. Place slices of bread on a baking sheet and toast for 5 minutes or until lightly brown. Brush each slice with olive oil mixture and bake for 1 more minute. Remove toast from oven and spread each slice with caponata.

Sprinkle with grated Parmesan cheese, if desired, and serve.

Makes 24 crostini

FOUR CHEESE CROSTINI

This little appetizer takes 10 minutes from package to plate.

Crostini:
Prepare the crostini using same ingredients and method as for Caponata recipe above.

Alternative Four Cheese Topping:

     1 1/2 cups Mozzarella cheese
     1 cup Fontinella cheese
     1/2 cup Parmesan cheese
     1/2 cup Romano cheese
     1 Tbs. toasted pine nuts

Preheat oven to 375 degrees. Bake crostini slices as above. In a large bowl, mix together all topping ingredients. Place a spoonful of cheese mixture on top of each toasted bread slice. Bake in oven for about 5 minutes, or until cheese melts.

Makes 24 crostini

FRIED MOZZARELLA STICKS

We love to serve our Marinara Sauce as a dip for these sticks. A firm style block of mozzarella works best here.

> 1/2 cup flour, mixed with a dash of pepper
> 2 eggs, beaten
> 1 1/2 cups Italian seasoned breadcrumbs
> 8 oz. mozzarella cheese, cut into 1/2-inch sticks
> 2 cups vegetable oil

Place flour, eggs and crumbs in 3 separate medium bowls. Dip the cheese sticks first into the eggs, then lightly dredge in flour. Repeat with eggs, then the crumbs, pressing thoroughly to coat the sticks. Place each stick on a cookie sheet and refrigerate or freeze at least one hour before frying. Just before serving, heat the oil in a deep, non-stick fry pan over medium. Fry cheese sticks until golden brown. Be careful not to cook them too fast or in overly hot oil. When cooked, remove to a paper toweled lined sheet. Serve immediately.

Serves 8 or 16 sticks

SICILIAN FRIED GREEN TOMATOES

Tomatoes are a staple in Sicily. Most villagers have access to a garden. At the end of the summer season, firm green tomatoes are a favorite side dish.

> 1 egg, beaten
> 1 Tbs. milk
> 1 cup Italian flavored bread crumbs
> 1/8 tsp. each black and cayenne pepper
> 1 tsp. garlic salt
> 3 to 4 firm green tomatoes, cored and thinly sliced
> Vegetable oil for frying
> Grated Parmesan cheese

In a small bowl, beat egg and milk. On a large plate, mix together breadcrumbs, peppers and garlic salt. Dip the tomato slices first in egg, then in crumb mixture. Coat both sides completely. In a large non-stick skillet, heat 1/2-inch oil in a large non-stick skillet over medium heat. Brown tomatoes on both sides. Remove and drain on paper towels. Place on serving platter, sprinkle with Parmesan cheese, and serve immediately.

Serves 6

FOCACCIA WITH OLIVES AND ROSEMARY

This famous Italian flat bread is usually served as an appetizer, along with extra-virgin olive oil for dipping.

2 cups warm water
2 tsps. dry instant yeast
4 1/2 cups all-purpose flour
2 tsps. salt
3 Tbs. olive oil
24 Greek-style brine cured olives, pitted and halved
1 Tbs. fresh rosemary, chopped
Additional extra-virgin olive oil for dipping

Place 2 cups warm water in large bowl. Dissolve yeast in water and let stand until it becomes puffy, about 10 minutes. Add flour and salt to yeast mixture and stir into a sticky and soft dough. Knead the dough on a floured surface until smooth and elastic, about 10 minutes, adding just enough flour to keep dough from sticking. Form a soft ball. Oil a large bowl and add dough, turning to coat. Cover with plastic wrap and let rise in warm area until doubled, about 1 1/2 hours. Punch down dough, knead lightly, form into a ball and return it to the bowl. Cover, and let rise in warm area until doubled, about 45 minutes.

Coat 15-inch x 10-inch baking sheet with 1 Tbs. olive oil. Punch down dough. Transfer to prepared sheet. Using finger-tips, press out dough to 13-inch x 10-inch rectangle. Let dough rest 10 minutes. Drizzle 2 tablespoons olive oil over dough. Sprinkle with olives and rosemary. Let dough rise uncovered in warm area until puffed and risen, about 25 minutes. Meanwhile, preheat oven to 475 degrees. Press fingertips all over dough, forming dimply indentations. Bake until brown and crusty, about 20 minutes.

Cool for 5 minutes before slicing. Serve warm, with a small pitcher of olive oil for dipping.

Makes 1 large focaccia

LEMON PAPRIKA BAR B Q CHICKEN

This marinade combination is a magically delicious tenderizer. Barbecues are a natural for summer gatherings, but in the beautiful January Arizona desert, they are real party pleasers. Whatever season you fire up your grill, this dish will be most welcome in a crowd.

> 12 pieces of chicken, any combination
> 3-4 fresh lemons, juiced
> 1/2 olive oil
> 2-3 garlic cloves, minced
> 2 Tbs. paprika
> 1 tsp. each salt and black pepper

Remove the skin from the chicken, then place the pieces in a large mixing bowl of cold water for about 10 minutes. Rinse off chicken, pat dry and set aside. In a small mixing bowl, mix together the lemon juice, olive oil, garlic, paprika, salt and pepper. Pour juice mixture onto chicken and coat each piece completely.

Refrigerate chicken in marinade for at least 1 hour. When ready, place the chicken on a well-greased grill. Grill until tender.

Serves 6

PERINI STYLE CHICKEN

This recipe comes from an old, now defunct neighborhood restaurant in the outskirts of Detroit. We originally got the recipe from the chef years ago and have enjoyed it now for four generations.

> 12 pieces of skinless chicken, in any combination
> 3 cups flour
> 4 Tbs. paprika
> 1 Tbs. garlic salt
> 1 tsp. black pepper
> 1 1/2 sticks margarine or butter
> 6 Idaho potatoes, peeled and quartered

Preheat oven to 300 degrees. Place chicken in a large bowl of cold water for about 10 minutes. Remove chicken and pat dry. In a shallow bowl, mix flour, paprika, garlic salt and pepper. Dredge chicken in flour thoroughly and set aside.

In a large non-stick skillet, melt 1 stick margarine over medium heat. Brown chicken until golden on both sides. It should not be cooked through. Set aside. Rinse potatoes and dredge in the same flour mixture. Brown potatoes until golden but not tender. Remove skillet from heat. Stir in 1 cup water to make a gravy. Arrange potatoes and chicken in a large baking dish. Cut up remaining margarine or butter and place pats around the chicken and potatoes. Pour the gravy on top, cover with aluminum foil and place in oven. Bake for 1 to 1 1/2 hours, depending on the size of the chicken pieces. Remove foil for last 30 minutes to brown both chicken and potatoes. Bring the dish to the table and serve immediately.

Serves 6

GRILLED MOZZARELLA SANDWICH

This fun version of a grilled cheese sandwich is one of my husband's favorites. Serve the sandwiches with a large platter of garden ripe tomatoes drizzled with your favorite olive oil.

8 slices Italian bread, (sliced to fit your appetite!),
    crust removed
8 oz. mozzarella cheese, sliced
1/2 cup milk
1 cup flour
1/2 cup Italian flavored bread crumbs
4 eggs, beaten
Salt and pepper to taste
1 cup olive oil

Place the cheese between two slices of bread. Lightly brush milk on both sides. Mix the crumbs and flour in a shallow plate. Pour eggs into a medium bowl. Lightly dredge the sandwiches in flour mixture, then slide them into the eggs, soaking the sandwiches on both sides. Season with salt and pepper.

In a large non-stick skillet, heat oil over medium. Fry sandwiches on both sides until golden brown. Drain on paper towels. Serve immediately.

Makes 4 sandwiches

SICILIAN FONDUE

In our family, Italian Fonduta is a great family participation event that we've enjoyed for years. Use this recipe as a basic guide, but have fun playing with different cheeses, textures and flavors.

1 garlic clove, halved
1 1/4 cups milk
8 oz. Mozzarella cheese, grated
8 oz. Provolone cheese, chopped
2 oz. Parmesan cheese, finely grated
2 tsps. cornstarch
3 Tbs. dry white wine
Breadsticks and bread, cut in chunks
1/4 lb. genoa salami, sliced
1/4 lb. Greek cured black olives

Rub the inside of a fondue pot with the garlic. Add the milk and heat over medium low until bubbling. Stir in all three cheeses and continue to heat until melted, stirring frequently. Blend the cornstarch with the wine, stir into the cheese mixture and cook, stirring, for a couple of minutes until thick and creamy. Serve with the breadsticks and bread for dipping and pass the salami and olives alongside.

Serves 4

MARSALA VEAL SCALOPPINE

For this dish, have your butcher pound the veal into extra thin, 1/2-inch scaloppine or cutlets.

> 3 cups fresh sliced white button, porcini, or
>   portabella mushrooms
> 1/2 cup shallots, thinly sliced
> 1/4 cup butter
> 8 slices veal scaloppine
> 1/2 cup flour
> 1/4 tsp. each salt and pepper
> 2/3 cup dry Italian Marsala wine
> 1/2 cup chicken broth
> 2 Tbs. fresh-chopped parsley

In a large non-stick skillet, sauté mushrooms and shallots in 2 tablespoons butter, over medium-high heat until tender, about 5 minutes. Remove from skillet and set aside. Pat veal with paper towel to remove excess moisture. On a large plate, mix together flour, salt and pepper. Dredge veal lightly in mixture. Add remaining butter to the skillet and sauté veal over medium low heat for 1-2 minutes on both sides, or until it is no longer pink. In the same skillet, add the rest of the butter and cook veal on low heat for about 1-2 minutes on both sides, or until no longer pink. Transfer meat to a warm serving platter and cover to keep warm. Add wine and broth to the skillet, stirring until liquid boils. Stir in mushrooms and parsley. Heat through and spoon the mushroom mixture over the veal.

Serves 4

VEAL SPIEDINI

Veal is the most widely used meat in Sicilian kitchens. This brochette recipe is easy for small get-togethers. Don't hesitate to double or even triple the recipe.

> 3-4 lbs. stewing veal, cut into 2-inch chunks
> 1/2 cup plus 2 Tbs. olive oil
> Salt and pepper to taste
> 3 cups Italian flavored bread crumbs
> 6-8 whole bay leaves, broken into quarters
> 1 whole yellow onion, quartered and separated
> 1/2 cup water
> 6 metal 10-inch skewers

Preheat oven 300 degrees. In a large mixing bowl, thoroughly coat the veal with the 1/2 cup oil. Season with salt and pepper. Place the breadcrumbs on a sheet of wax paper. Roll veal cubes in breadcrumbs to completely coat. Skewer the cubes, alternating with the onion and bay leaves. Place side by side on a large baking sheet. Cover meat and bake for 2 hours.

In a small bowl, stir together 1 crumbled bay leaf, water and remaining olive oil. Baste the veal with this every 30 minutes, turning the skewers over as you baste. Uncover for the last 30 minutes to brown the veal. Serve warm.

Serves 4

PASTA AND SICILIAN TOMATO SAUCE

Aunt Sarah's scrumptious non-cook
sauce recipe is absolutely the quickest
ever Sicilian tomato sauce. If you
assemble all the sauce ingredients
ahead of time, it can be whipped up
as the noodles cook.

8 oz. mostaccioli
1/4 cup plus 1 Tbs. olive oil
1/4 cup pine nuts
1/4 cup Parmesan cheese, grated
2 garlic cloves, minced
2 cups fresh basil leaves
1/4 cup olive oil
1 1/2 lbs. ripe tomatoes, roughly chopped
1/2 tsp. each salt and pepper
Additional Parmesan cheese

Cook pasta in boiling water adding 1 tablespoon olive oil to
the water. As pasta cooks, place nuts, cheese and garlic in a
food processor and blend to chop. Add basil and remaining oil,
process to blend. Add tomatoes and pulse until you have a
chunky consistency. Season to taste with salt and pepper. Place
sauce mixture in a medium saucepan and warm to bubbly.

When pasta is just al dente, drain and place in a warm serving
bowl. Top with the sauce and sprinkle with Parmesan cheese.
Serve immediately.

Serves 4

STUFFED BEEF ROLL 'BRUSHA LUNA'

My mom is always very proud of her dinner presentations. She believes that the eyes are the first to eat a feast. "Brusha-luna?" I have yet to find it in any Italian dictionary. (Could be that Mama May made up that title.) The only clue so far is that slices of the roll look like a "luna" or moonburst. Moon or no moon, this Sicilian party dish is a winner.

1/4 lb. ground beef
1 garlic clove, minced
1 egg, beaten
3 Tbs. Parmesan cheese, grated
1/4 cup Italian flavored bread crumbs
1/2 14-oz. can green peas, drained
2 Tbs. Italian parsley, chopped
Salt and pepper to taste
1-2 lbs. lean beef steak, in 1 piece, pounded 1/2" thick
1/2 lb. Genoa salami, chopped
1/2 lb. prosciutto, thinly sliced
3 whole hard-boiled eggs
3 Tbs. olive oil
1 onion, chopped
1 cup Chianti wine
1 Tbs. tomato paste
1 cup water
Heavy twine

In a large mixing bowl, combine ground beef, garlic, egg, cheese, breadcrumbs, peas, parsley, salt and pepper and set aside. Place salami and prosciutto on top of pounded beef slice. Spread ground beef mixture on top. Place the whole hard-boiled eggs end to end over the narrow part of the beef slice.

Starting from the narrow end carefully roll up the beef slice. Tie it securely with the twine.

In a large non-stick skillet, over medium heat, heat the olive oil and sauté the onion for 2-3 minutes, or until soft. Brown the beef roll on all sides. Pour in the wine and cook until the wine evaporates. Stir together the tomato paste and water and add to the skillet. Cover the skillet and simmer until the roll is tender, about 1-1/2 hours. Let meat stand for about 5 minutes. Slice roll into 1/2-inch pieces. Each slice should have a lovely "moonburst" egg slice.

Serves 4

SICILIAN STUFFED ARTICHOKES

Artichokes are usually served as an appetizer, but with my family's way of preparing them, this dish can be served as an entrée. Note that with the healthy amount of Parmesan cheese used, no extra salt is needed.

> 4 large artichokes
> 2 cups Italian flavored bread crumbs
> 1/2 lb. Parmesan cheese block, cut into 1/2 inch chunks
> 3-4 cloves of garlic, minced
> 3/4 cup extra-virgin olive oil
> Black pepper

Preheat oven to 350 degrees. With a scissors, cut the tips from each artichoke. Rinse artichoke under cold water, and spread leaves open. Over a sheet of wax paper, take each artichoke and stuff each leaf with the breadcrumbs, pressing in crumbs. Press the cheese chunks randomly into the leaves. Sprinkle each with garlic and press all remaining ingredients into the artichoke.

Place the artichokes in a medium sized deep baking pan with about 3-inches of water. Drizzle olive oil over each artichoke and season each with pepper. Cover with aluminum foil and bake for 1 to 1/2 hours, or until artichoke leaves begin to separate from the center. Baste with pan juices every 1/2 hour. Uncover pan the last 10 minutes to brown the tops. Serve immediately.

Serves 4

HAZELNUT PANNA COTTA

Torrone is an Italian nougat bar made with egg whites, toasted almonds and honey that is flavored with essences, spices or liqueurs. It can be found in most Italian groceries and deli's. (see pg. 16 for directions)

> 1 envelope unflavored gelatin
> 6 Tbs. milk
> 3 cups heavy cream
> 6 oz. Torrone
> cup honey
> 1 cup hazelnuts, chopped
> 6-8 soufflé molds or custard cups, lightly buttered

In a small mixing bowl, sprinkle gelatin over milk and let stand for 10 minutes. In a medium saucepan combine heavy cream, Torrone and honey. Bring to a boil, stirring to dissolve ingredients. Remove from heat and stir in gelatin and milk, stirring until gelatin dissolves. Pour mixture into cups; chill until set, about 2 hours. To unmold, dip cups in warm water for about 5 seconds. Then invert onto individual plates and serve topped with chopped hazelnuts.

Serves 6-8

RICOTTA CHEESE PIE

My Aunt Rose rarely gave out her recipes. However, this is one of her specialties that has been passed down to us. The almonds, citron and creamy ricotta filling are a wonderful combination.

Pastry:
> 2 cups flour
> 1/3 cup powdered sugar
> 1/2 tsp. baking powder
> 1/2 tsp. salt
> 1/2 cup butter, cut in small pats
> 2 Tbs. brandy
> 1/3 cup water

Filling:
> 2 lbs. part-skim milk ricotta cheese
> 1 cup sugar
> 4 eggs
> 1 Tbs. flour
> Grated zest of 1 lemon
> 2 Tbs. almonds, chopped
> 2 Tbs. citron, chopped
> 1 tsp. vanilla
> 1 egg, slightly beaten

Preheat oven to 400 degrees. For the pastry, combine the flour, sugar, baking powder, salt and butter in a food processor. Pulse the processor until the mixture resembles coarse crumbs. Add the brandy and water; pulse until the mixture sticks together and forms dough. Shape dough into a ball.

Between two floured sheets of waxed paper, roll two-thirds of dough into a 13-inch circle. Place in a 10-inch spring-form pan.

Roll remaining pastry between waxed paper into a 10-inch circle. If dough is too soft, chill until firm, then cut into 8 equal strips.

For the filling, place ricotta, sugar, eggs, flour, lemon zest and vanilla in the bowl of a food processor and blend until smooth. Add nuts and citron; process just until combined. Pour mixture into pastry-lined pan. Remove any excess dough around sides of pan, leaving a 1/2-inch of pastry border above the cheese mixture. Arrange pastry strips in a lattice pattern over top.

Bake for 10 minutes, then lower heat to 350 degrees and bake for an additional 45 minutes. Cool and serve.

Serves 10

MELONE CAKE ROLL

Cantaloupe is featured in this summertime family favorite, and can be made a couple of hours in advance. Serve with a scoop of gelato alongside it for extra zip.

> 4 cups flour
> 1 tsp. baking powder
> 1/4 tsp. each ground nutmeg and salt
> 4 eggs, separated
> 1/2 tsp. vanilla
> 1/3 cup sugar plus an additional 1/2 cup
> Powdered sugar
> 1 cup lemon low-fat yogurt
> 1/2 small cantaloupe, peeled, seeded and finely chopped

Preheat oven to 375 degrees. Grease and flour a 15-inch x 10-inch x 1-inch baking pan. In a medium bowl, combine flour, baking powder, nutmeg and salt. In another medium bowl, beat egg yolks and vanilla with an electric mixer for 5 minutes or until thick and lemon colored. Gradually add 1/3 cup sugar, beating until sugar dissolves. Thoroughly wash beaters. In a large bowl, beat egg whites until soft peaks form or tips of the peaks curl. Gradually add remaining 1/2-cup sugar and continue beating until stiff peaks form or tips of the peaks stand straight up. Fold yolk mixture into egg whites. Sprinkle flour mixture over egg mixture and fold very gently until combined. Spread evenly in prepared pan. Bake for 12-15 minutes. While cake bakes, sift powdered sugar onto a clean kitchen towel. When cake is firm, remove from the oven and immediately loosen edges. Turn cake out onto the prepared towel. Starting with a narrow end, roll warm cake and towel together. Allow cake to cool in the towel.

Stir together yogurt and melon. When cake is cool, unroll it and spread melon mixture leaving a 1-inch border on the edges. Reroll cake, cover, and refrigerate until serving time. Slice and serve with your favorite gelato or ice.

Serves 10

CHAPTER 3

SUNDAYS AND SPECIAL OCCASIONS
SIMPLY SPECIAL DISHES

For we Italians, every Sunday or holiday is typically linked to some religious belief. Our family also celebrated the traditional holidays in grand style. We would don new clothes to visit the relatives. These events were not for the faint of heart. Sometimes 60 'close family' members would show up for a full day of social bonding at the table. And it sure wasn't limited to just 2 days a year. Any birthday, anniversary, baptism or Sunday was an excuse to gather up the troops, set the table and eat together for hours. What follows are easy ways to entertain your own clan be it a party of 8 or 80.

MINESTRONE SOUP 'THE BIG SOUP'

In our family, seasonal vegetables and herbs surrounding the shrine to Our Lady in the back yard were picked and used to grace the table in dishes sometimes as simple as a delicious bowl of soup. Meat was often scarce in the homes of my Italian peasant relatives. No one seemed to mind when a huge pot of piping hot hearty soup was brought to the table filled with sweet garden vegetables, beans and pasta. Warm, crusty loaves of bread for dipping and a big dish of aged Parmesanto sprinkled on top made minestrone one big soup to look forward to. For us, it's still a welcome centerpiece.

> 2 Tbs. olive oil
> 2 garlic cloves, minced
> 1 medium onion, chopped
> 3-14 1/2 oz. cans of vegetable broth
> 1 cup carrots, sliced
> 1-10 oz. package frozen lima beans
> 1 medium potato, peeled and quartered
> 1-14 1/2 oz. can red kidney beans, drained
> 1-8 oz. can tomato sauce
> 1 small tomato, diced
> 1 Tbs. fresh parsley, chopped
> 1 Tbs. fresh or dried basil
> 1 cup seashell macaroni
> Grated Parmesan cheese

In a large soup pot, heat oil over medium. Sauté garlic and onion in oil until tender. Stir in all other ingredients, except the pasta. Heat to boiling, then reduce heat to simmer, cover, and cook for 20 minutes. Stir in pasta. Cover and simmer another 10-15 minutes or until pasta is tender. Be careful not to overcook the pasta, or it will fall apart in the soup. Bring to the table immediately with a bowl of grated Parmesan cheese.

Serves 6

PEA SOUP

Mama May perfected this soup and streamlined the cooking process. Delicious and hearty, this soup can be made in advance and stored in the freezer for an impromptu party. Remember, the pasta often swells and swallows the soup! Setting aside some of the liquid helps to give it the perfect consistency.

> 1 large onion, chopped
> 2-14 1/2 oz. cans green peas
> 1-8oz. can tomato sauce
> 4 Tbs. olive oil
> Salt and pepper
> 1 Tbs. sugar
> 1 cup small seashell macaroni

Place the onion and peas in a blender, adding one can at a time. Add the juice from the peas slowly so that the blender container does not overflow. Blend until peas are completely pureed. In a medium–size saucepan, stir together the pureed pea mixture, tomato sauce and olive oil, along with 3-8oz. cans of water. Season with salt, pepper and sugar. Heat to boiling over medium heat, stirring often, then reduce heat, cover and cook for about 20 minutes. Remove about 2 cups of pea soup and set aside. Add pasta, cover and simmer for 10-15 minutes, or until pasta is tender. When pasta is cooked, stir in the 2 cups reserved soup.

Serves 6

SAUSAGE AND PEPPERS

Grilling sausage in the dead of winter in Detroit was never questioned in my household. That memorable open-flame taste was well worth standing in the freezing cold!

3 medium onions, sliced
3 sweet green peppers, sliced
4 garlic cloves, chopped
2 Tbs. each olive oil and balsamic vinegar
1/8 tsp. black pepper
6 fresh Italian sausage links
6 long hard Italian or sub rolls

Prepare grill to medium-hot temperature. In a large bowl, mix together all ingredients except the sausages and bread. Place 1/2 of the mixture in an 18-inch square sheet of heavy-duty aluminum foil. Repeat with remaining mixture and additional foil. Fold two opposite sides of foil over; fold edges together 3 times to seal; fold other two ends over 3 times. Grill packets over indirect coals on covered grill for 45 minutes. Grill sausages turning occasionally, over medium-hot coals on covered grill for at least 15-20 minutes. When cooked, slice rolls and fill with a sausage link and vegetables.

Serves 6

PASTA CROWN

Here is the Sicilian king of pasta dishes. This stunning crown has enhanced many of our holiday and Sunday tables.

4 cups Spaghetti Sauce (see traditional sauce pg. 125)
1 lb. farfalle pasta
2 Tbs. olive oil

1/2 lb. lean ground beef
1 cup mushrooms, thinly sliced
1/2 medium red onion, chopped
1/2 small carrot, thinly sliced
3 large eggs, lightly beaten
1 cup fresh basil, chopped
1 cup Mozzarella cheese, shredded
1/2 cup Provolone cheese, shredded
3/4 cup Parmesan cheese, grated
1/2 cup frozen green peas
4 fresh basil sprigs

Preheat oven to 350 degrees. In a medium saucepan, bring spaghetti sauce to a simmer over low heat. Lightly oil a large round glass casserole dish. Cook pasta until al dente tender, drain and set aside. Do not rinse. Heat 1 tablespoon oil in a medium non-stick skillet and brown ground beef. Drain meat and set aside. Wipe skillet clean, add remaining oil and cook mushrooms, onion and carrots over medium heat for about 10 minutes until tender. Add ground beef, stir, and cook for 5 minutes. Set mixture aside. In a large bowl, stir together eggs, vegetables, basil, mozzarella, provolone, 1/2 cup Parmesan and 1 cup sauce. Stir in pasta and peas until pasta is completely coated. Spoon into casserole dish, and gently press down into dish. Cover and bake 45 minutes. Remove from oven and let stand, covered, for about 5 minutes. Meanwhile, heat remaining sauce until bubbly. Uncover casserole and carefully turn upside down onto a large serving platter. Spoon sauce over top. Sprinkle with remaining Parmesan. Decorate platter with basil sprigs.

Serves 8

CALAMARI

Calamari and octopus are often served during the holidays, especially on Christmas Eve, when the stars of the table are usually fish and pasta.

> 1 lb. fresh squid, (separated), washed and patted dry
> 2 garlic cloves, halved
> 1 1/2 cups corn oil plus 1/2 cup olive oil, for frying
> 1/2 cup all-purpose flour
> 1/2 tsp. salt
> 1 Tbs. freshly ground black pepper
> 1/4 tsp. cayenne pepper
> 1 large egg, beaten
> 1 Tbs. fresh lemon juice
> 1 cup Italian-flavored bread crumbs
> 2 lemons, cut into wedges

Cocktail sauce:
> 1/2 cup ketchup
> 1 tsp. prepared horseradish or more to taste

Soak squid in a large bowl of lightly salted water for 20 minutes. In a medium saucepan, heat the corn and olive oil. Cut squid into 1/2-inch pieces. On a large plate, mix together flour, salt and both peppers. In a small bowl, stir together the egg and lemon juice. Place breadcrumbs on a large plate. Lightly flour, shaking off excess. Then dip squid into egg mixture and coat with breadcrumbs. Fry garlic and squid 3 to 5 minutes or until golden brown. Remove and drain on paper towel lined sheet. Serve immediately with lemon wedges and cocktail sauce on the side.

For cocktail sauce, mix together ketchup and horseradish.

Serves 6

BREADED EGGPLANT

This classic eggplant dish can stand alone as an appetizer or serve as a hearty vegetable side dish to accompany almost any meat.

> 1 large eggplant, thinly sliced lengthwise
> Salt
> 2 eggs, beaten
> 1/2 cup flour
> 1 cup Italian-flavored bread crumbs
> Olive oil, for frying
> Parmesan cheese

Lightly sprinkle each piece of eggplant with salt and place in a colander in the sink for about 1 hour allowing eggplant to drain. Press down on the slices to remove any remaining moisture. Pat each slice with a paper towel. Place eggs in a shallow bowl. Place flour and crumbs on two separate large plates. Dredge eggplant slices first in flour, then dip into eggs. Firmly press crumbs into both sides. In a large non-stick skillet, heat about 2 inches of oil over medium heat. Fry slices until golden brown on both sides, about 5 minutes on each side. Drain on paper towels. Sprinkle with Parmesan cheese and serve warm.

Serves 4

BREAD SALAD

Leftover bread is never ever wasted in a Sicilian house. Next time you're left with an old loaf, try this comforting salad. The herbs and oil soften the bread and make such a satisfying treat out of leftovers.

For the salad:
> 1 loaf of day-old Italian bread, about 4 cups,
>> in 1-inch cubes
> 2 medium ripe tomatoes, roughly chopped
> 2 garlic cloves, finely chopped
> 1 medium green bell pepper, chopped
> 1 small celery stalk, chopped
> 1/2 small red onion, chopped
> 1/3 cup fresh basil, chopped
> 2 Tbs. fresh Italian parsley, chopped

For the dressing:
> 1/3 cup extra-virgin olive oil
> 1/3 cup red wine vinegar
> 1/2 tsp. salt
> 1/4 tsp. black pepper
> Dash of Italian dried mixed seasoning

In a large bowl, mix together all the salad ingredients. Place dressing ingredients in a shaker bottle with top. Shake well and pour over bread mixture, tossing gently. Cover and refrigerate for at least 1 and up to 5 hours.

ZUCCHINI BOATS

These spicy little vegetarian boats can be assembled up to one day in advance.

> 4 to 6 small zucchini, washed and halved lengthwise
> 1/4 cup olive oil
> 1/2 small onion, minced
> 1 garlic clove, minced
> 1/4 tsp. crushed red pepper flakes
> 1-8oz. can of Italian (stewed) tomatoes
> 4 mushrooms, sliced
> 1/4 tsp. salt
> 1/8 tsp. black pepper
> 1/2 tsp. each dried oregano and basil
> 2 Tbs. red wine
> 1 cup Italian-flavored bread crumbs
> 1/2 cup Parmesan cheese, grated

Scoop out the centers of the zucchini, leaving a 1/2-inch border. Roughly chop and set aside. Rub the shells on both sides with oil. Preheat oven to 350 degrees. In a large non-stick skillet, heat remaining oil over medium high. Add onion, garlic, and crushed red pepper to pan and sauté over medium heat, until soft, about 5 minutes. Add the scooped out zucchini, tomatoes, mushrooms, salt, pepper, oregano and basil. Cook for 1 minute, then stir in wine. Cook another minute and remove from heat. Stir in the breadcrumbs and cheese. Fill the zucchini boats and arrange in an oiled baking dish. Bake about 30 minutes, or until zucchini is soft. Serve immediately.

Serves 4

STUFFED PEPPER CUPS

These are a convenient and delicious party food especially when a hungry crowd gathers for a big buffet.

> 6 large green bell peppers, cored, seeded and rinsed
> 1 Tbs. olive oil
> 1 lb. lean ground beef
> 1 box Spanish rice
> 2 eggs, beaten
> 1 cup breadcrumbs
> 1 can tomato soup

Preheat oven to 300 degrees. Heat the olive oil in a large skillet over medium heat. Cook, but do not brown the meat. Drain the fat and set meat aside. Prepare Spanish rice according to box directions and set aside to cool. In a large mixing bowl, beat together eggs and breadcrumbs. Thoroughly blend in meat and rice. Fill the peppers and place in an oiled deep baking dish. Spoon tomato soup over the top. Cover and bake for 1-1/2 hours or until peppers are soft. Serve immediately.

Serves 6

CITY CHICKEN

We've always called this 'mock chicken.' The cracker meal gives the meat a crunchy bite which is like crispy chicken skin.

> 2 lbs. stewing veal, cut in 1-inch cubes
> 1 lb. pork, cut in 1-inch cubes
> Salt
> 2 cups cracker meal
> 1/2 Tbs. garlic, minced
> 1 egg, beaten
> 4 Tbs. butter or margarine
> 8-10 6-inch wooden skewers

Preheat oven to 300 degrees. Rinse meat under cold water, pat dry with paper towels and lightly sprinkle with salt. Set aside. Place the cracker meal and eggs in a shallow dish. Alternate the veal and pork cubes on the skewers, leaving a 1-inch border on both sides. Dip the skewers into the egg, then coat with the cracker meal. In a large non-stick skillet, melt the butter on low heat, add garlic, and brown the skewers on all sides but do not thoroughly cook. Place meat in a deep, glass, baking dish. Cover and bake for 1 hour. Uncover and bake for about 1/2 hour more or until golden brown. Serve immediately.

Serves 6-8

ROSEMARY ROASTED PORK

Pork loves rosemary! That's probably why so much of both find their way to Sicilian kitchens. Less is more here. A few herbs turn this simple roast into a feast.

2 lbs. pork tenderloin
4 Tbs. fresh rosemary
4 tsps. olive oil
Kosher salt
Black pepper to taste

Preheat oven to 400 degrees. Line a baking tray with foil. Spray it with cooking spray and place in oven. Remove fat from pork and butterfly the meat; Cut it nearly in half lengthwise; open the pork like a book. Pound it flat with the palm of your hand or a mallet. Chop rosemary and rub pork with olive oil, salt and pepper, then sprinkle rosemary on both sides. Remove baking tray from oven and place pork on hot tray. Place in oven and roast 15 minutes. Remove and let stand for about 5 minutes and then carve on an angle against the grain. Serve immediately

Serves 4

AGLIO OLIO CHICKEN

Your house will smell of sweet garlic, pungent rosemary and roasted chicken. Welcome in the flavors of Sicily.

1 5-6 lb. whole roasting chicken
1 Tbs. fresh rosemary, chopped
8 garlic cloves, crushed
2 medium red onions, quartered
2 whole garlic heads
2 tsps. olive oil
1 large loaf crusty Italian bread

Preheat oven to 450 degrees. Remove and discard giblets and neck of chicken. Rinse chicken under cold water. Pat dry and trim excess fat. Starting at neck cavity, loosen skin from breast and drumsticks by inserting fingers and gently pushing fingers between the skin and meat. Place rosemary and crushed garlic beneath the skin of breast and drumsticks. Lift wing tips up and over back; tuck under chicken. Place chicken, breast side up, on a broiler pan. Cut a thin slice from end of each onion. Remove white papery skins from garlic heads, but do not peel or separate cloves. Cut tops off garlic heads, leaving root end intact. Insert meat thermometer into meaty part of thigh, making sure not to touch bone. Roast at 450 degrees for 30 minutes.

Brush onions and garlic heads with olive oil and arrange around chicken. Reduce oven temperature to 350 degrees and roast for an additional 1 hour and 15 minutes, or until meat thermometer registers 180 degrees. Cover chicken loosely with foil; let stand 10 minutes. Discard skin from garlic. Squeeze roasted heads of garlic to extract pulp and serve warm on bread alongside the chicken.

Serves 8

CHICKEN PICCATA

Here's a typical Sunday favorite that needs almost no time to prepare.

> 4 skinless, boneless chicken breasts,
>   pounded to 1/2-inch
> 1/2 tsp. salt
> 1/4 tsp. black pepper
> 2 Tbs. flour
> 1 Tbs. olive oil
> 2 garlic cloves, minced
> 1 cup chicken broth
> 3/4 tsp. dried rosemary, crushed
> 1 Tbs. lemon juice
> 1 Tbs. butter or margarine
> Fresh Italian parsley

Season chicken with salt and pepper. Place flour on a plate and dredge chicken. Heat oil in a large non-stick skillet over medium heat and sauté garlic. Add chicken broth, rosemary, lemon juice and butter. Raise heat to medium-high, and sauté chicken breasts until golden brown and firm, about 5-6 minutes. Serve immediately, topped with a fresh sprig of Italian parsley.

Serves 4

LEMON ICE

After a big, summer Sicilian supper, this melts in the mouth. Divine!

> 2 cups each sugar and water
> 1 Tbs. lemon peel, grated
> 1 cup fresh lemon juice
> Fresh mint sprigs

Heat water and sugar to boiling in a saucepan; reduce heat. Simmer, uncovered, 5 minutes; remove from heat. Stir in lemon peel and juice. Cool 10 minutes and freeze in an ice cream maker or cool to room temperature and pour into a ungreased 9-inch x 5-inch x 3-inch loaf pan. Freeze 2 hours. Stir mixture; freeze about 1 more hour longer, stirring every 30 minutes, until firm. Stir again before serving. Serve in chilled dessert dishes and place a fresh mint sprig on top.

Makes 1 quart

ALMOND COOKIES

Almonds are abundant throughout Sicily. Lots of the harvest is processed into various Italian liqueurs but there are always plenty to use for desserts such as this crunchy treat.

3 cups slivered raw almonds
3 jumbo egg whites
1 1/2 cups granulated sugar
1 tsp. powdered sugar
1/4 tsp. almond extract or 1 tsp. amaretto liqueur
Additonal granulated sugar

Heat oven to 350 degrees. Spread raw almonds in ungreased shallow pan. Toast ten minutes or until golden brown, stirring occasionally. Cool. Set aside 1/2 cup nuts. Reduce oven to 300 degrees. Line cookie sheet with parchment paper or grease and flour cookie sheet. Place almonds in a food processor or blender. Process to finely grind, but be careful not to make a paste. In a medium bowl, beat the egg whites with an electric mixer on high speed until stiff. Stir in almonds and sugars, and almond extract. Drop by teaspoonfuls, about 2 inches apart, onto prepared sheet. Sprinkle with granulated sugar and remaining toasted almond slivers. Bake 20 to 25 minutes until light golden brown. Cool and remove from cookie sheet.

Makes 4 dozen

PIZZELLE

These wafer-thin anise cookies have been a holiday tradition for decades. You'll need a pizzelle iron which can be purchased in kitchen specialty shops and some Italian groceries. There are both manual and electric irons to choose, depending on your ambition.

2 cups all-purpose flour
1 cup sugar
3/4 cup butter or margarine
1 Tbs. anise extract
2 tsps. baking powder
4 large eggs, beaten
1/2 cup powdered sugar

Lightly grease pizzelle iron and heat according to manufacturer's directions. Mix all ingredients in a large mixing bowl, except the powdered sugar, and whisk until smooth. Drop a scant tablespoon of batter onto the iron and close cover. Wait about 30 seconds or until golden brown, then carefully remove pizzelle from iron and cool. Sift sugar over cooled pizzelle. Serve within a day or store in a covered container for up to one month.

Makes 3-4 dozen

PIÑALOTTE: SWEET PUFF PASTRY

These beautiful little puffs of dough are often displayed in Sicilian bakery shop windows. These are by far our most popular holiday dessert and we use a big mountain of them as a centerpiece.

Dough:
>   10 eggs, lightly beaten
>   2 tsps. baking powder
>   1 tsp. vanilla
>   1/2 cup sugar
>   4 cups flour
>   Crisco for frying

To assemble:
>   16 ounces honey
>   2 cups sugar
>   2-8 oz. Hershey's chocolate bar with almonds,
>   coarsely chopped
>   Candy sprinkles

Heat a deep fryer to 365 degrees. In a large bowl, combine eggs, baking powder, vanilla, sugar, and flour. Stir and lightly knead mixture to form a soft dough. Turn out onto a floured surface and knead, adding more flour if necessary to make a smooth dough that is not sticky. Roll the dough into a 1/2-inch macaroni shaped tube. Cut the tube into 1/4-inch pieces. Place on a large cookie sheet and dust with flour. Have a large brown paper bag at hand. To cook piñalotte, place dough in a fryer basket and fry for 1 1/2 minutes. Remove and place in the bag. Shake to remove the oil and transfer to a bowl. Assemble immediately.

In a small saucepan, combine honey and sugar and heat over low until sugar dissolves. Add to the bowl of fried dough and mix until well coated. Scoop into balls and dust with chocolate and candy sprinkles. Pile high into a triangle to form a mountain or using a damp hand, spread into a glass baking dish. When mixture cools, cut into 3-inch squares.

Makes 3-3 1/2 dozen

CHAPTER 4

TRADITIONS, SOUPS AND ROMANTIC PARTY FOODS

Sicily is the birthplace of many of our modern traditions, especially Italian weddings, where confetti and candied almonds are tossed after the ceremony. "Sweet boxes," another typical wedding offering, originated in 15th century Italy. These symbolized good fortune and were exchanged by both families. In time, the boxes were made of porcelain and become known as the bonboniere. Today, the boxes contain 5 sugared almonds symbolizing health, wealth, happiness, fertility and long life, and are personalized by a small folded card with the bride and groom's first names and the wedding date. Roles have reversed since the 15th century, now the bonboniere are often given to guests as thank-you gifts.

Ancient Romans would bake a cake made of wheat or barley and break it over the bride's head as a symbol of her fertility. It became tradition to pile up several small cakes, one on top of the other, as high as they could, and the bride and groom would kiss over the tower and try not to knock it down. If they were successful, it meant a lifetime of prosperity.

THE NOBLE BEAN

For centuries, fagioli have reigned supreme for Italians.
We've learned to make magic with fava beans, chickpeas,
lentils, red and white kidney beans, just to name a few. Beans
are not a recent passion. Apicius, the recorder of many
sophisticated classical Roman recipes, wrote of an aromatic
vegetable soup eaten by the aristocracy. The Roman emperor,
Heliogabalus, offered his guests a dish of lentils, seasoned with
precious stones!

What follows are a few humble and frugal recipes filled with rich
flavor and imaginative seasonings. They have become part of my
family's culinary heritage and are still made on a regular basis.

PASTA E FAGIOLI

Make this hearty soup at least one day ahead so that the beans
really have a chance to soak up the flavors.

> 12 ounces dry red kidney beans
> 1 large onion, diced
> 5 Tbs. olive oil
> 1 8 oz. can tomato sauce
> 1 Tbs. sugar
> 1 1/2 cups small shell pasta
> Salt and pepper to taste

Rinse the beans several times, removing any stones. Place in a
large soup pot and cover with water. Soak overnight, adding
additional water if the beans absorb it all.

To cook the beans, bring the soup pot to a boil and simmer 4-
6 hours or until beans are tender. Remove 1/2 of the cooked
beans along with some of the water, and mash beans with a

fork. For a smoother texture, place in blender and puree to smooth. Return mixture to the same pan, and simmer over low heat. In a large skillet, sauté the onion in the oil until onion is tender, about 5 minutes. Add to the beans, along with the tomato sauce and sugar. Season to taste with salt and pepper. Simmer over low heat for another 2 hours, adding water if needed. Soup should be creamy, but not too thick. Twenty minutes before serving, increase the heat to medium high. When the soup is almost at a boil, add the pasta. Lower the heat and simmer until pasta is tender, stirring often. If soup starts to stick to the pot or appears too thick, add water. Serve hot.

Serves 8-10

THREE BEAN SOUP

Mamma May's original recipe. This soup began as a minestrone, but over the years, preparation time had to be shortened and adjustments made due to busy schedules. Still healthy and hearty, this soup can be prepared quickly and is great as an appetizer or a whole dinner if served in an Italian bread bowl.

> 2 quarts chicken broth
> 3-4 heads of garlic, peeled and minced
> 2 Tbs. olive oil
> 3 medium potatoes, peeled and diced
> 1/2 lb. green beans
> 3 carrots, sliced
> 1-15 oz. can red kidney beans, drained
> 1-15 oz. can garbanzo beans, drained
> 1 medium onion, diced
> 1/2 zucchini, sliced
> 3-4 garlic heads, minced
> 1-6 oz. can tomato paste
> 1 Tbs. dried basil
> Dash of black pepper

1/2 cup Parmesan cheese, grated
1/2 cup dried or fresh parsley

In a large saucepan, bring broth to a boil over medium heat. In a small skillet, sauté garlic in olive oil over medium heat until softened, about 5 minutes. Add it to the broth along with potatoes, green beans, carrots, both canned beans, and onion, then cook for 1 hour, simmering over medium low heat. Add zucchini and continue to cook for 1/2 hour. In a small bowl combine tomato paste, basil, pepper, parmesan cheese, and parsley, making a paste. Add these ingredients to soup and simmer for about 1/2 hour more.

Serves 4-6

Which shape pasta for the soup?

My dad, a first generation Sicilian, was the first of 9 kids. Sundays in his house meant chicken soup. In the early days, all 9 kids fought to choose which noodle graced the soup that week. Finally in desperation, grandma stopped the fights with a brilliant move. Bingo! All 9 types of pasta always went in! Now, Mama May adds just tiny orzo which is less complicated but still produces the best Italian chicken soup ever.

TRADITIONAL CHICKEN SOUP

1 whole chicken, cut up
6-8 carrots, chopped
4 stalks celery, chopped
1 large onion, quartered
2 fresh tomatoes, or 1-12oz. can tomato sauce
1 Tbs. mixed pickling spices
Salt and pepper to taste
1 1/2 cups orzo pasta
Parmesan cheese

Wash chicken parts and soak in lightly salted water for about 5 minutes. Meanwhile, fill a large soup pot about half full with water and place over medium-high heat. Add chicken and bring to a boil. Cook for about 10 minutes, skimming off any foam as it appears. Add carrots, celery, onion, tomatoes and spices. Heat to a boil again over medium-high heat, uncovered. Reduce the heat to a slow but steady simmer. Partially cover and cook for 2 hours. Strain the broth through a fine sieve and remove chicken and carrots and set aside. Discard the rest of the contents in the sieve. Mash carrots and add back to the clear broth. Remove chicken from bones, cut into pieces and add back to soup. Bring soup to boil, add pasta and simmer over low-medium heat, stirring often to prevent sticking, for about 15 minutes or until pasta is cooked. Serve sprinkled with cheese.

Serves 6-8

ITALIAN WEDDING SOUP

Traditionally, this soup is always served as one of several first courses at Sicilian weddings.

8 cups homemade chicken broth
3/4 pound each ground beef and pork
8 eggs
1 cup dry bread crumbs
2 tsps. dried basil
1 tsp. dried parsley
1 1/2 cups grated Parmesan cheese
2 medium heads escarole, cleaned and chopped

In a large, heavy soup pot, bring the broth to a boil over medium heat.

In a large bowl, combine the meats, 3 eggs, crumbs, basil, parsley and 1/2 cup cheese. Mix well and form bite-size balls. Drop the balls into the broth. Then add escarole. Cook until meatballs rise to the top, and escarole has wilted about 6 to 7 minutes. In another bowl, mix together remaining eggs and cheese. Pour mixture into soup, stirring continuously, until the egg is cooked, about 2-3 minutes. Serve sprinkled with additional Parmesan cheese.

ROASTED VEGETABLES

This family classic is a versatile antipasto. Feel free to substitute vegetables that fit the season. During the summer, try this with garden tomatoes, marinated Italian olives and fresh mozzarella.

1 large red onion, cut into 1-inch pieces
2 heads garlic, peeled
2 red bell peppers, cut into 1-inch squares
1 eggplant, cut into 1-inch pieces
1 1/2 lbs. small new potatoes, cut in half
8 lbs. baby carrots
1/2 lb. green beans, cut in half
1/2 cup olive oil
2 1/2 tsps. salt
1/4 tsp. ground pepper
2 Tbs. fresh herbs--rosemary, thyme, parsley, chopped
    or 1 Tbs. dried herbs
1/4 cup dry white wine
1/4 pound feta cheese, crumbled
3 Tbs. fresh basil or parsley, chopped

Put one oven rack on the upper third of the oven, and the other on the lower third of the oven and heat to 500 degrees.

In a large bowl, combine all the vegetables and oil. Season with salt pepper, and herbs, mixing well. Divide the vegetables between two large roasting pans and spread each batch in even layers. Sprinkle with wine. Roast the vegetables for 15 minutes. Stir, then switch the pans from one rack to the other. Repeat after another 15 minutes. Divide the cheese and fresh herbs between the two pans and mix well. Rotate the pans again and continue roasting until the vegetables are brown, 15 to 20 minutes longer. Transfer vegetables to a large serving dish and sprinkle with basil or parsley. Serve hot or at room temperature.

Serves 8

POOR MAN'S CAVIAR

I know it's a stretch to equate eggplant with caviar. But what's in a name and who cares? It's always welcome in our house because it's an easy crowd pleaser for any season. The ricotta cheese gives the Sicilian version of this classic its twist.

> 1 large eggplant
> 1/4 cup red onion, finely chopped
> 1/4 cup Italian parsley
> 3 Tbs. olive oil
> 1 garlic clove
> 2 Tbs. lemon juice
> 1 Tbs. balsamic vinegar
> 2 Tbs. ricotta cheese

Preheat oven to 400 degrees. Place the eggplant in a baking dish and pierce the skin several times. Bake for 40 minutes, or until soft. When cooled, scoop out the pulp and place in a blender with all other ingredients. Chill overnight.

Serves 4-6

OLIVE PASTE

In Sicily, groves of hearty olive trees can be found everywhere. The harvest is enormous and for centuries people have looked to simple ways to use olives—marinated, minced as a season-ing, and or mashed into a tasty paste, such as this one that our family spreads on toasts.

1/2 pound green Sicilian olives,
  or black Greek olives, pitted
2 garlic cloves
2 sprigs Italian parsley
2 tsps. capers
1/4 tsp. dried oregano
2 tsps. dried rosemary
1/2 tsp. thyme
2 Tbs. lemon juice
1/4 cup olive oil
1/2 tsp. crushed red pepper flakes
2 Tbs. red wine vinegar

Blend all ingredients in a blender and blend to form a smooth paste. Refrigerate in a sealed container until use.

Serves 6

SICILIAN HUMMUS

Our Armenian Cousin Anne gave us this recipe. We added a few of our Sicilian standby ingredients to create this global hummus. Serve it as a dip with raw vegetables, bread sticks or flat bread.

1-16 oz. can garbanzo beans
1/2 cup pine nuts
1/3 cup fresh lemon juice
1/2 tsp. basil
1/4 cup fresh Italian parsley, chopped
1/2 tsp. cumin
2 garlic cloves
1/2 cup olive oil
1/2 tsp. salt
1/4 tsp. crushed red pepper flakes

Place all ingredients in a blender and blend to form a smooth paste. Refrigerate in a sealed container for up to 3 days.

Serves 6-8

RISOTTO FORMAGGIO

Always cook Italian arborio rice until just tender, but still quite firm to the bite.

2 Tbs. olive oil
1 medium onion, chopped
1 cup Arborio rice
1/4 cup dry white wine
3 1/2 cups homemade or purchased chicken broth
1/2 cup ricotta cheese
1/2 cup mozzarella cheese, shredded
1/2 cup Parmesan cheese, shredded
1 Tbs. each Italian parsley and basil, chopped

In a large saucepan, heat oil over medium-high. Sauté the onion in oil until soft, about 5 minutes. Stir in rice and cook about 5 minutes, stirring, until rice is translucent. Stir in wine and cook another few minutes until wine is completely absorbed. Meanwhile, heat chicken broth in the microwave until hot. Slowly add about 1/2 cup of the broth at a time to the rice until all the broth is absorbed, and the rice is tender and mixture is creamy. Stir in the cheeses. Pour into a large serving bowl and sprinkle top with fresh parsley and basil.

Serves 2-4

PASTA CON PESCE

Christmas Eve is the night fish and pasta reign deliciously supreme. Meat is normally avoided. Since the sea around Sicily is abundant with fish, I think there are more recipes for pasta with seafood than all the fish to be found!

PASTA CON SARDE

Pasta con Sarde is much more delectable than you'd think. Although grandmother used fresh sardines, we Americans have learned to substitute friendly canned sardines. Buy the best quality imported ones you can find that are usually packed in extra-virgin olive oil.

1/2 cup olive oil
1/2 tsp. crushed red pepper
1 fennel bulb, trimmed and diced
2 -3.6 oz.cans sardines, drained
1/4 cup kalamata black olives, pitted and chopped
1/4 cup fresh Italian parsley, chopped
1 tsp. dried basil
1 lb. spaghetti

In a large saucepan, heat oil and red pepper over high heat. Add fennel, lower heat to medium and cook for about 5 minutes or until soft. Add sardines, olives, parsley and basil. Cover and simmer for 5 minutes, stirring gently, until fennel is very tender. If mixture seems too dry, drizzle on a little more olive oil. Cook pasta until just al dente tender. Just before draining, scoop out about 1/2 cup water and set aside.

Toss pasta with sardine mixture, adding some of the reserved water to moisten, but not enough to make the sauce runny.

Serves 4-5

LINGUINE WITH CLAM SAUCE

Here is the king of all Sicilian seafood pasta dishes. Treat yourself to fresh linguine when making this one.

> 2 Tbs. margarine
> 1 small garlic clove, finely chopped
> 1 Tbs. flour
> 1 cup clam juice
> 1/4 cup parsley, chopped
> Pepper to taste
> 1/2 tsp. dried thyme
> 1 cup minced clams, fresh or canned
> Tabasco sauce
> 1 pound fresh linguine
> Parmesan cheese, freshly grated

In a large saucepan, heat the margarine over medium heat. Add the garlic and cook for one minute. Stir in the flour and cook for 2 minutes, stirring constantly. Add the clam juice and stir until sauce thickens, about 2 minutes. Add the parsley, pepper and thyme. Simmer gently for 10 minutes, stirring occasionally. Add minced clams and cook only until clams are heated. Taste and add a dash of Tabasco. Cook linguine in a large kettle of boiling, salted water until just al dente tender. Drain and place in saucepan. Coat with sauce and turn out into a large serving bowl. Serve sprinkled with Parmesan cheese.

Serves 3-4

LINGUINE WITH RED CLAM SAUCE

Our family often craves red sauce! If it's a traditional seafood pasta night with friends we'll choose this alternative to the white sauce above.

> 1-35 oz.can (35 ounces) whole peeled tomatoes
> 1 can (6.5 to 8 ounces) whole clams or minced clams
> 2 Tbs. olive oil
> 2 large garlic cloves, minced
> 3 Tbs. Italian parsley, chopped
> Crushed red pepper flakes
> Salt and freshly ground black pepper, to taste
> 1 lb. linguine, cooked

Drain the tomatoes, reserving the juice. Drain the clams, reserving 1/4 cup of the clam juice. In a large saucepan, heat olive oil over medium heat until hot. Add the garlic and cook, stirring, until golden. Be careful not to burn it! Stir in tomatoes, breaking them up with the side of a wooden spoon; stir in the clam juice. Bring the mixture to a simmer, then lower heat to medium-low and cook, stirring occasionally, 5 minutes, until heated through. Stir in the clams and parsley and simmer for another 5 minutes. Taste and season the sauce with a dash of red pepper flakes, salt, and lots of freshly ground black pepper. If necessary, thin the sauce with some of the reserved tomato juice. Keep warm, stirring, over very low heat. Serve over hot linguine.

Serves 3-4

CALAMARI IN TOMATO SAUCE

Serve this as an appetizer or main course depending on the rest of the menu and the appetite of the crowd. Simmering the calamari over low heat ensures that it won't get rubbery.

2 lbs. fresh squid sacs, cleaned
4 cups tomato sauce
1 cup Chianti wine
2 Tbs. fresh lemon juice
1 Tbs. olive oil
2 large garlic cloves, chopped
1 Tbs. fresh basil, chopped
1 tsp. each black pepper and crushed red pepper
1/2 pound thin spaghetti
1/3 cup Romano cheese

Cut squid into 1/4-inch slices and set aside. In a medium saucepan, combine all ingredients except pasta and cheese. Simmer on medium-low heat for about 30 minutes or until wine has evaporated. Add the squid. Continue to simmer for another 30 minutes, stirring occasionally. Calamari is done when it is opaque in color and plump. Cook spaghetti until it is just tender. Drain and pour sauce over spaghetti. Toss to mix well and sprinkle with Parmesan cheese. Serve hot.

Serves 4-6

DOLCE MEMORIES

Sicilian weddings are the height of friends loving friends. With that in mind, the wedding tray is the ultimate sharing of "dolci" or the Sicilian celebration of life. This is not taken lightly! Silver trays are teetering with every manner of hand-made cookie. In our family, teen members are chosen to parade and serve these extravaganzas to usually more than 300 guests. The trays are so laden that younger kids can hardly see over them! Front and center are powdery crescents, sesame fingers, rich chocolate and aromatic vanilla wafers sitting next to creamy filled cannoli. Baked morsels cuddle with piles of crisp fried dough fingers and colorful candy coated silver twists make the trays sparkle. Scattered all around the platters are the 'cunvathes' or traditional candy coated almonds. It's a vision! Here's a handful of what you might find.

ITALIAN WEDDING COOKIES

> 1 1/2 cups unsalted butter
> 3/4 cup powdered sugar, plus 1/3 cup, for rolling
> 3/4 tsp. salt
> 1 1/2 cups finely ground blanched almonds
> 5 1/2 tsps. vanilla extract
> 3 cups sifted all-purpose flour

Preheat oven to 325 degrees. Cream butter in a bowl. Gradually add powdered sugar and salt. Beat until light and fluffy. Add almonds and vanilla. Blend in flour gradually and mix well. Shape into crescents using about 1 teaspoon for each cookie. Place on ungreased cookie sheets, and bake for 15 to 20 minutes. Do not brown. Cool slightly, then roll cookies in the extra powdered sugar.

SFINCI

Pronounced sfeen-ge, these little beignets or fritters are heavenly light.

> 1 lb. ricotta cheese
> 1/2 cup sugar
> 4 eggs
> 2 tsps. baking powder
> 2 tsps. vanilla
> 1 Tbs. ground cinnamon
> 1 cup flour
> 1 1/4 cups canola oil for frying
> Honey
> Powdered sugar

In the large bowl of an electric mixer, beat together ricotta, sugar and eggs. When blended, add baking powder, vanilla, and cinnamon. Gradually add flour, making a thick batter. Add a little more flour if mixture appears too thin. In a large skillet or deep fry pan, heat oil to 375 degrees. Drop several teaspoonfuls of batter into oil. Fry until puffy and golden brown, about 3 minutes. Remove with slotted spoon and place on paper towel lined sheet. When ready to serve, drizzle with honey and sift sugar over the top.

Makes 3 dozen

CANNOLI

It's hard to manage 2 quarts of milk in a standard double boiler! We always fashion our own with a large skillet filled with water. We simply place a saucepan over the skillet and 'ecco!'

Filling:
>   2 quarts whole milk
>   3/4 cup cornstarch
>   5 cups sugar
>   3 cinnamon sticks
>   1 zest of lemon
>   2 Tbs. vanilla extract
>   1 1/4 cups chopped Hershey chocolate bar with nuts

In the top of a large double boiler, place milk, cornstarch and sugar. Place over the water bath over medium heat. Add cinnamon sticks, zest and vanilla, and cook, stirring often, until thick, about 30-45 minutes. Place filling in bowl and cool in refrigerator. When cold, fold in 3/4 cup chocolate pieces and refrigerate until ready to use.

Cannoli shells:
>   8 cups sifted all-purpose flour
>   6 Tbs. sugar
>   1/4 cup ground cinnamon
>   8 Tbs. crisco
>   2 eggs, beaten
>   1/4 cup red table wine
>   1 1/3 cups water
>   2 1/2 cups canola oil
>   Powdered sugar

In a large mixing bowl, combine flour, sugar and cinnamon. Using a pastry blender, add Crisco to dry ingredients and blend until crumbly. Make a well in the center of the bowl and add eggs, wine and water as needed to form a firm pie dough. Wrap dough and refrigerate for 30 minutes. Remove dough from refrigerator and roll into a 12-inch rectangle, on a lightly floured surface. The dough should be just over 1/8-inch thick. Cut dough into nine 4-inch squares. Round off the two opposite corners of each square using a rolling pin. Lightly grease the cannoli tubes. Twist each square around a tube, joining the non-rounded corners; press with fingertips to seal securely. In a large, deep skillet, heat oil to 375 degrees. Fry each pastry covered tube about 3 minutes or until golden brown, using tongs to turn frequently. Remove from oil; drain well on paper towels. Cool slightly; then remove metal tubes. Place pastry shells on rack to cool completely.

To finish the cannoli:
Fill each pastry tube will filling. Dip each end in remaining chocolate pieces. Just before serving, sift powdered sugar over tops.

Makes 48-50 cannoli

ITALIAN RICOTTA COOKIES

2 cups sugar
1 cup margarine or butter, softened
1-15 oz. container ricotta cheese
2 tsps. vanilla
2 large eggs
5 cups flour
2 Tbs. baking powder
1 tsp. salt

Icing:

1 large orange
3 cups powdered sugar
Orange-colored sugar

Preheat oven to 350 degrees. Lightly grease a cookie sheet. In large bowl of an electric mixer beat together sugar and butter on low speed until blended. Increase speed to high and beat until light and fluffy, about 5 minutes. Reduce speed to medium and beat in cheese, vanilla and eggs until well combined. Reduce speed to low and add flour, baking powder and salt. Beat until a soft dough has formed. Drop level tablespoonfuls, about two inches apart, on a prepared cookie sheet. Bake 15 minutes or until cookies are lightly golden. Cookies should be soft. Remove cookies from the sheet with a spatula. Cool and prepare icing.

Icing:
In a small bowl, scrape the orange to remove the zest. Squeeze the orange into the same bowl. You will need about 1/2 cup of juice. Gradually add juice and the sugar and mix at low speed until smooth. Icing should not be runny; add more sugar if needed to produce a firm icing. Spread icing on cookies with a knife and sprinkle with orange colored sugar. Set aside to allow icing to dry completely, about 1 hour.

Makes 6 dozen

SESAME COOKIES

Baker's ammonia is very strong, so take care not to inhale while mixing, or when opening the oven door!

 9 cups flour
 2 1/2 cups sugar
 6 Tbs. powdered vanilla
 2 cups Crisco
 3 large eggs, beaten
 1 1/2 cups milk
 3 Tbs. Baker's ammonia
 2 egg whites
 2 cups hulled sesame seeds

Preheat oven to 350 degrees. Lightly grease a cookie sheet. This is best mixed by hand so make sure you have lots of space to work on. Pour the flour onto the center of a large cutting board. Mix in sugar, 4 Tbs. powdered vanilla and cut in the Crisco using a pastry blender. Make a well in the middle of the mixture and gradually add eggs, milk and ammonia. Dough should now feel and look like soft cookie dough. If it is too dry, add a little more milk; if too sticky add a little more flour.

Roll dough out by hand to form a long sausage shape, about 1-inch round. Cut into 3-inch pieces then roll again into sausages about as thick as an index finger. In a small bowl, mix the egg whites with 2 tablespoons water. In a small bowl, mix the sesame seeds with remaining 2 Tbs. powered vanilla. Dip the cookie first into the egg wash, then roll in sesame seeds until completely covered. Place about two inches apart on prepared pan and bake 15-20 minutes or until lightly golden brown. Remove cookies from sheet with a spatula and cool.

Makes 12 dozen

MAKING SESAME COOKIES

CHERRY ALMOND "S" COOKIES

Almond flavoring is often used with these cookies but you may divide the cookies and choose to flavor them separately with cherry, lemon, vanilla or chocolate. Don't forget! Like the sesame cookies, be aware that baker's ammonia is super strong. Do not inhale it while mixing or opening the oven door!

> 9 cups flour
> 4 Tbs. powdered vanilla
> 2 1/2 cups sugar
> 2 cups Crisco
> 3 large eggs, beaten
> 1 1/2 cups milk
> 3 Tbs. Baker's ammonia
> 1/2 cup hot water
> Icing (see p.80)
> Colored candies or sugar (optional)

Preheat oven to 350 degrees. Lightly grease a cookie sheet. On a flat surface or large cutting board mix together flour, powdered vanilla, sugar, and Crisco. Make a well in the center of dough and gradually add the beaten eggs and milk. Mix the ammonia and hot water in a small cup and stir until the ammonia melts. Mix it into the dough. Dough will feel soft like cookie dough. Roll dough into a long sausage shape, about 2-inches thick. Then cut dough into 3-inch lengths. Now roll by hand into shapes of balls, circles or "S". Place about 2 inches apart on prepared pan and bake 10-15 minutes or until the bottom of the cookies are light golden brown. Remove cookies from the sheet with a spatula and cool. Prepare icing using your favorite flavor and spread on cookies, using a dull knife. Sprinkle with colored candies or sugar if desired. Set aside to allow icing to dry completely, about 1 hour.

Icing:

      2 lbs. powdered sugar
      6 Tbs. almond flavoring
      2 Tbs. cherry flavoring
      5-6 Tbs. water

Beat all ingredients in a small bowl on low speed, or by hand until smooth in firm spreading consistency.

Makes 12 dozen

CHAPTER 5

ROMANCE-COOKING FOR TWO

Cooking for family and friends is a wonderful experience that involves giving from the heart. Meals designed for two can be just as special. These Italian recipes for two are simple yet designed for a fun time in the kitchen, without leftovers! So select your menu; put on some music and tune into a great movie after dinner.

'THE BIG NIGHT'
"You'll like it so much you'll go back for seconds."

Starring Minnie Driver, Ian Holm and Isabella Rossellini
(Rated R)

A dinner of first courses!
This is the pasta lover's ideal dream meal.

THE MENU

Asparagus Pasta Salad
Smoked Salmon with Ricotta Lasagne
Noodle Pudding

ASPARAGUS PASTA SALAD

Here's a really simple but impressive alternative to mixed greens.

> 1/2 lb. bow tie pasta
> 1/2 lb. fresh asparagus, cut into 1-inch slices
> 4 vine-ripe fresh tomatoes, quartered
> 1/2 cup Balsamic vinaigrette
> Pecorino cheese, grated
> 2 tsps. olive oil

Cook pasta until just tender and drain. Toss with oil and chill in large serving bowl. Toss with tomatoes, vinaigrette and asparagus. Serve sprinkled with cheese.

Serves 2

SMOKED SALMON WITH RICOTTA LASAGNE

This is an elegant twist on the classic dish.

> 1/2 lb. lasagne noodles
> 1/4 cup olive oil
> 1/4 cup Italian parsley, finely chopped
> 1 Tbs. fresh oregano
> 2 Tbs. fresh basil, chopped
> 1/2 lb. ricotta cheese
> 1/4 lb. smoked salmon
> 3-4 tomatoes, thinly sliced
> 1/2 cup mozzarella cheese, shredded

Preheat oven to 375 degrees. Cook lasagne according to package directions. In a medium mixing bowl, blend together parsley, oregano, basil, and ricotta cheese. Lightly oil an 8-inch x 10-inch glass baking dish and alternate layers of noodles, cheese mixture, salmon, and tomatoes in the dish. Top with mozzarella cheese and cover with aluminum foil. Bake for 40 minutes, or until bubbly. Remove foil for last 5 minutes to brown top. Allow lasagne to stand at least 10 minutes before serving.

Serves 2

PASTA PUDDING

Start with pasta; end with pasta. Now that's our kind of dessert!

> 4 oz. wide egg noodles
> 1/2 cup cottage cheese
> 2 oz. cream cheese
> 1/2 cup sour cream
> 1/4 tsp. vanilla extract
> 1/4 cup sugar
> 1 large egg, beaten
> 2 Tbs. butter, melted

Topping:
> 1/2 cup graham cracker crumbs
> 2 Tbs. butter, melted
> 2 Tbs. sugar
> 1/4 cup whipped cream

Preheat oven to 350 degrees. Grease a small casserole dish, or two small oven-safe custard cups. Cook noodles until just tender and drain. Blend together cottage and cream cheeses until smooth. Mix in sour cream, vanilla, sugar and egg. In a medium bowl, mix together noodles, cheese mixture and butter, coating noodles completely. Place in prepared dish. For topping, mix together all ingredients and spread over noodles.

Bake for 15 minutes, then lower oven to 325 and bake for an additional 45 minutes. Cool completely before serving. Top with whipped cream.

Serves 2

BAKED POLLO ITALIANO

The garlicky dressing makes this no-fuss dish jump with spicy flavor. Make it when prep time is short and appetites are hearty.

> 4 pieces chicken, any desired cut
> 1/3 cup Wishbone Italian dressing,
> 3 medium potatoes, cut into small chunks
> 3 carrots, thinly sliced
> 2 celery stalks, roughly chopped

Place chicken and dressing in a medium, shallow, glass baking dish, coating chicken thoroughly. Cover and marinate in refrigerator for 3 and up to 24 hours. Preheat oven to 425 degrees. Add vegetables to marinade and bake, basting occasionally, for 40 minutes or until chicken is thoroughly cooked and potatoes are tender. Season with salt and pepper to taste and serve.

Serves 2-3

PASTA WITH PEARS AND SWEET POTATO

It takes longer to say this pasta than to cook it!

 1 large sweet potato
 6 oz. fresh spinach fettuccine
 2 Tbs. brown sugar
 2 Tbs. olive oil
 2 tsp. butter
 1 tsp. water
 2 Tbs. Parmesan cheese, grated
 1/3 cup Pecorino cheese, shredded plus 1 oz. shaved
 1/2 firm ripe pear, peeled and cut into matchsticks
 1 Tbs. fresh parsley, chopped
 Freshly ground pepper

Preheat oven to 400 degrees. Place the sweet potato on a tray and bake for about 20 minutes; or microwave for 6 minutes, until tender. When cool, peel and cut into 1/2-inch slices. Place on a lightly oiled cookie sheet and set aside. Bring a large saucepan of salted water to the boil and cook fettuccine until just al dente tender. In a medium saucepan, combine sugar, oil, butter and water. Cook over medium heat, stirring constantly, until sauce is smooth and bubbly, about 2 minutes. Set aside 2 Tbs. of sauce. Brush the rest over the sweet potatoes and sprinkle with Parmesan cheese. Broil until lightly brown. When pasta is ready, drain and toss with reserved sauce and 1/3 cup Pecorino. Place pasta in serving dish and top with potato slices and pears. Serve immediately sprinkled with shaved Pecorino cheese, parsley, and pepper.

Serves 2

LEMON VEAL PICCATA AND RISOTTO

The term 'piccata' means sharp or tangy. This is a light and zesty dish.

> 1/2 lb. boneless round rump veal, trimmed and
>   cut into 1-inch cubes
> 1 Tbs. flour
> 1 tsp. beef-flavored bouillon granules
> 1/2 tsp. paprika
> 1 small sprig parsley, chopped
> 14 tsp. dried rosemary
> 1/8 tsp. ground black pepper
> Cooking spray
> 2 medium carrots, cut into thin strips
> 1/4 cup dry white wine
> 1/4 cup water
> 1 Tbs. lemon juice
> 2 cups cooked risotto or long grain rice

In a heavy-duty zip top plastic bag, combine meat, flour, bouillon, paprika, parsley, rosemary and pepper. Seal bag and shake to coat. Spray a large non-stick skillet with cooking spray and heat over medium. Brown the veal. Add carrots, wine, water and lemon juice and bring to boil, stirring constantly. Cover, reduce heat, and simmer 40 minutes. Serve over risotto.

Serves 2

GARLIC BROCCOLI

This is really at home with any white meat such as chicken or pork. Use the greenest and freshest veggies you can find.

Olive oil
2 cups fresh broccoli flowerets
1 garlic clove, minced
2 Tbs. green onions, chopped
1/4 cup chicken broth
1/8 tsp. each salt and pepper
1 Tbs. Parmesan cheese, grated

Heat a large non-stick skillet over medium-high heat and film the bottom with oil. Add broccoli, garlic, onions, broth, salt and pepper. Cover and cook until crisp tender, about five minutes. Place in a serving bowl, and serve sprinkled with cheese.

Serves 2

GINGER MARMALADE GLAZED BEETS

Use small to medium beets for this. The larger ones can be a little woody and take much longer to prepare.

1 lb. fresh beets, scrubbed
3 Tbs. orange marmalade
1/4 cup unsweetened apple juice
1 Tbs. lemon juice
1 tsp. crystallized ginger, minced
2 Italian parsley sprigs

Place beets in a medium saucepan in water to cover. Heat to boiling, cover pan, and cook for 30 minutes or until beets are tender. Drain and place beets in cold water. When cool enough to handle, trim roots and rub skins to peel. Cut cooked beets into 1/4-inch slices and set aside. Combine marmalade, apple juice, lemon juice, and ginger. Mix beets and marmalade mixture in a medium saucepan. Reheat over medium, stirring, until beets are warmed through and coated with sauce. Serve topped with Italian parsley.

Serves 2

MARINATED CRAB SALAD

When fresh crab is available this salad makes a wonderful lunch or dinner.

6 iceberg lettuce leaves, washed
8 endive leaves, washed
1/2 lb. fresh lump crabmeat
1/2 small purple onion, chopped
1/2 small red pepper, cut into strips
1/4 small yellow pepper, chopped
2 stalks celery, chopped
1/4 cup olive oil
2 Tbs. white vinegar
1 Tbs. Dijon mustard
1/4 tsp. dried thyme
1/2 cup garbanzo beans
2 fresh Italian parsley sprigs

Chill lettuce leaves in paper towels. Mix together all remaining ingredients except parsley. Chill for 3 hours. Line 2 salad plates with lettuce. Arrange 4 endive leaves on each plate in the shape of a flower. Spoon crab mixture over endive and serve topped with parsley.

Serves 2

BASIL SUGAR SNAP PEAS

Be careful not to overcook the peas! They should have a definite crunch.

    1 Tbs. olive oil
    1/2 lb. sugar snap peas
    2 Tbs. fresh basil, chopped
    2 tsps.. lemon zest
    Salt and white pepper to taste
    2 lemon wedges

Heat oil in a medium non-stick skillet over medium-high. Stir-fry peas for 3-4 minutes or until crisp-tender. Add remaining ingredients except lemon wedges and stir-fry for 1 minute. Serve immediately with lemon wedges.

Serves 2

CHICKEN SCALOPPINE

Classically, this scaloppine is made with veal, but the prosciutto and spices really work well with lighter meats like chicken.

    1 small egg white
    1 Tbs. water
    1/2 cup Italian flavored bread crumbs
    1 Tbs. fresh parsley, chopped
    1 garlic clove, minced
    1/8 tsp. freshly ground black pepper
    2 boneless skinless chicken breast halves,
        slightly pounded to flatten
    Salt
    2 thin slices prosciutto
    1/4 lb. orzo pasta
    1 Tbs. olive oil

Parmesan cheese, grated
2 lemon wedges

Heat broiler. Whisk egg white and water together in a shallow dish. Combine breadcrumbs, parsley, garlic, and pepper in another shallow dish. Season chicken lightly with salt and press 1 prosciutto slice on each piece. Dip chicken first in egg white mixture, then press in crumbs. Prepare orzo pasta according to directions; drain and set aside. As pasta cooks, place chicken on broiler rack and drizzle with 1/2 tsp. olive oil. Broil 3 minutes; turn and drizzle with remaining oil. Broil about 3 minutes more or until chicken is firm and just opaque in center. Place chicken on bed of orzo pasta, sprinkle with Parmesan cheese and serve with lemon wedges on the side.

Serves 2

SAUTÉED ZUCCHINI

When available, use garden-fresh tender, young zucchini and basil.

2 Tbs. olive oil
3 small zucchini, sliced 1/2 inch thick
1/2 tsp. fresh basil, chopped
1 garlic clove, minced
Salt and pepper to taste
Parmesan cheese, grated

Heat the oil in a medium non-stick skillet over high heat and sauté zucchini for 3 minutes. Add basil, garlic, salt and pepper; and cook 1 minute, stirring carefully. Sprinkle with cheese and serve immediately.

Serves 2

PESCE PER DUE

It's worth it to scout out a good fish market so you can use fish that is still flappin' fresh with no fishy smell. Here's my favorite, mouth-watering fish for two dish.

2 halibut or grouper fillets, about 1 lb.
2 Tbs. butter or margarine, melted
2 Tbs. lemon juice
1/8 tsp. lemon-pepper seasoning
1 garlic clove, minced
Dash of paprika
1 Tbs. fresh chopped Italian parsley
Salt and pepper to taste
1 purple onion, sliced
2 lemon wedges

Preheat oven 350 degrees. Place fish fillets in a lightly greased 13-inch x 9-inch x 2-inch baking pan. Pour melted butter and lemon juice over fish. In a small bowl, combine remaining ingredients except onion and lemon and sprinkle on fish. Top with onion slices. Cover with aluminum foil and bake for 20-25 minutes. Uncover and heat oven to broiler setting. Broil fish for 3-4 minutes until lightly brown and easily flaked with a fork. Serve with lemon wedges.

Serves 2

ANGEL HAIR PASTA WITH SHRIMP AND ASPARAGUS

8 jumbo fresh shrimp, unpeeled
6 oz. angel hair pasta
1/4 cup olive oil
2 garlic cloves, minced
2 medium shallots, chopped
6 stalks asparagus, cut into 2-inch pieces
1/2 small tomato, peeled, seeded and diced
4 medium fresh shiitake mushroom caps, sliced
1/4 tsp. salt
1/8 tsp. dried crushed red pepper
1/2 cup dry white wine
1 Tbs. fresh basil, chopped
1 Tbs. fresh oregano, chopped
1 Tbs. fresh thyme, chopped
1 Tbs. fresh Italian parsley, chopped
1/4 cup Parmesan cheese, freshly grated

Peel and devein shrimp; set aside. Cook pasta until just al dente tender. Drain and set aside. Heat a large non-stick skillet over high heat for 1 minute. Add oil and heat 10 seconds. Stir in shrimp, garlic and shallots. Cook, stirring constantly, 2-3 minutes or until shrimp turn pink. Add asparagus, tomato, mushrooms, salt and red pepper. Stir in wine, scraping bottom of pan to loosen any particles. Add pasta, and then toss gently with the herbs. Sprinkle with cheese and serve immediately.

CINNAMON CROSTINI WITH BALSAMIC BERRIES

This makes a great dessert of course, but consider just how wonderful it would be for a Sunday breakfast.

> 1 pint strawberries, cleaned and halved
> 1/2 cup sugar
> 2 Tbs. butter
> 2 1/4-inch slices crusty Italian bread
> 1/4 tsp. ground cinnamon
> 1 Tbs. balsamic vinegar
> 1 Tbs. water
> 1/4 cup whipping cream
> 2 fresh mint sprigs

In a medium bowl, mix together the berries with 1/4 cup sugar and set aside for 30 minutes. The sugar will melt and form a syrup. Preheat oven to 350 degrees. Butter the bread and dust lightly with cinnamon and remaining sugar. Bake until lightly toasted, about 5 minutes. While toast is baking, stir vinegar and water into berries and taste for sweetness. Sprinkle them with a little sugar if they seem too tart.

With a hand whisk or beater, whip cream until stiff and set aside. Place the toast on 2 plates and spoon 1/2 of the berries and marinade over each one. Serve topped with whipped cream.

Serves 2

STUFFED PEACHES

This Sicilian classic proves that almonds and peaches are a heavenly combination.

> 2 medium ripe, unpeeled peaches, halved and pitted
> 2 Tbs. apricot preserves
> 2 Tbs. Amaretto liqueur
> 2 coconut cookies or macaroons, coarsely crushed
> 1/4 cup whipped cream

Preheat oven to 350 degrees. Film a small baking dish with cooking spray. Halve peaches and remove pits, but leave unpeeled. Arrange peaches in dish and spoon 1/2 Tbs. apricot preserves and 1/2 Tbs. crushed cookies into each cavity. Drizzle 1/2 tablespoon Amaretto on each peach half and lightly spray with cooking oil. Bake for 15 minutes, then remove from oven and cool 12-15 minutes. Serve warm with whipped cream.

Serves 2

CHAPTER 6

BREAKFAST AND BRUNCH
TEMPTING MORNING MEALS

Buon giorno, Italian style! There is more to breakfast than a quick cup of coffee and a bagel. Simple or elaborate, a little imagination can turn simple ingredients into heart-winning meals. You won't have to visit Italy to create these dishes. Just use easily found ingredients that capture the Italian spirit.

BEVERAGES:

The Coffee Bar - Caffé, which not only means coffee, espresso and cappuccino, but also means coffee bars. It is an essential way to start off your day, so brewing the perfect cup means coffee that is rich in color without leaving a bitter and unpleasant aftertaste.

Espresso must be brewed in an espresso machine in order to force steam to flow through the coffee beans and give that distinctive taste. Use only espresso-style blends of coffee beans and grind just before brewing. A shot of espresso is a measurement and refers to the small shot or cup that is used to make it.

Steamed milk can be done by inserting your espresso machine's steam nozzle into a small pitcher of milk, and heating the milk to 150 degrees.

CAPPUCCINO

Cappuccino is named for the Capuchin monks. The coffee resembles the monk's robe and the white foam symbolizes his hair.

> 1 shot of espresso
> Steamed milk
> Cocoa powder or ground cinnamon
> Sugar
> Sugar or cinnamon stick

Brew the espresso and pour into a coffee cup. Slowly pour on steamed milk. Sprinkle the top with either cocoa powder or cinnamon. Serve with sugar, or cinnamon sticks to swirl in the coffee.

Serves 1

CAFFÉ LATTE

Caffé latte is one third espresso and two-thirds milk

>   1 shot of espresso
>   Steamed milk

Brew the espresso and pour it into a warm coffee cup. Slowly pour in the steamed milk, using a spoon to slow the milk from mixing with the coffee. Serve with sugar.

Serves 1

DRINKS AND SPIRITS

AMARETTO CAFFÉ

Amaretto liqueur is an almond flavor liquor actually made from apricot pits that add a sweet and nutty flavor to coffee.

>   1 cup brewed black coffee
>   1 oz. Amaretto liqueur
>   1 dollop whipped cream
>   Maraschino cherry

Fill a coffee cup with hot black coffee. Stir in Amaretto. Top with whipped cream and a cherry.

Serves 1

BELLINI

This drink was created in Venice and named after the artist, Jacopo Bellini.

> 2 cups of peach puree or peach nectar, chilled
> 2 tsps. fresh lemon juice
> 4 cups of chilled sparking wine, such as Asti-Spumante.
> Mint sprigs

Chill champagne glasses in freezer for at least 1 hour. When ready to serve, remove glasses from freezer. Fill each glass with equal amounts of peach puree or nectar and 1/2 tsp. of lemon juice. Slowly pour wine into glasses and gently stir. Top each glass with a mint sprig.

Serves 8

SICILIAN SMOOTHIE

This is the ultimate warm weather breakfast or afternoon snack. Sprinkle the top with cinnamon or Ghiradelli chocolate shavings.

> 2 shots espresso
> 4 scoops vanilla ice cream
> 1 banana
> 2 scoops ice

Thoroughly blend all ingredients in a blender until creamy. Serve immediately in chilled tumblers.

Serves 2

SICILIAN SUMMER SODA

Torani is a wonderful source for fruity and nutty flavors that can be added to coffee or soda, and can be purchased by the bottle in most grocery stores.

1/2 cup Torani Strawberry syrup
4 cups sparkling water or club soda
4 cups ice

In a large pitcher, stir together syrup, soda and ice. Stir well and serve.

Serves 4

EGGS I UOVI

My Uncle Tom, quite the character, sold fruit and vegetables door-to-door from his truck when I was a kid. Tom's favorite breakfast was to take one of his fresh from the farm eggs and poke a hole in each end. Then, tilting his head back just so, he'd slurp 'em down raw. Personally, I do suggest cooking eggs before serving them! Here are our family's favorite Sunday eggs. For large groups, these recipes can be held in a chafing dish, buffet style.

Try this twist on the American standard as is or between two pieces of freshly toasted Italian bread.

> 1/2 lb. of Maple-smoked bacon
> 1 dozen large eggs
> 1/2 cup milk
> 1/2 tsp. salt
> 1/4 tsp. black pepper
> 4 Tbs. butter
> 1/2 medium red onion, chopped
> 2 Tbs. fresh basil, chopped
> 4 small, ripe Roma tomatoes, diced

Fry bacon strips until brown and crisp. Drain on paper towels and set aside. In a large bowl, whip all 12 eggs, milk, salt and pepper. Melt butter in a large non-stick skillet over medium low heat. Add onion and sauté until is very clear, about 5 minutes. Stir in egg mixture with a wooden spoon, stirring constantly. Add tomatoes and bacon, cooking until eggs are soft and fluffy. Place on serving platter and serve garnished with basil.

Serves 6

SICILIAN CHEESE SCRAMBLE

Slow stirring over low heat makes all the difference with scrambled eggs.

    1 dozen eggs
    1/2 cup whipping cream
    1/2 cup each Mozzarella and Parmesan cheeses, shredded
    4 Tbs. butter
    Salt and pepper to taste
    Fresh parsley

In a large bowl, beat eggs. Slowly add cream and cheeses. In a large non-stick skillet melt butter over low heat. Add the egg mixture and cook, stirring consistently, until eggs are fluffy, about 3 to 4 minutes. Season with salt and pepper and serve on warm plates, topped with a sprig of parsley.

Serves 5-6

PASTA AND SCRAMBLED EGGS

Everyone loves pasta so why not be bold and combine it with scrambled eggs? Trust us! The small egg bits in the pasta are rustic but fabulous!

    1 dozen large eggs
    2 Tbs. heavy cream or Mascarpone cheese
    1 cup Parmesan cheese, freshly grated
    2 Tbs. butter
    2 Tbs. olive oil
    3 garlic cloves, minced
    1/4 pound thinly sliced bacon, cut into 1/2 inch strips
    1/4 cup. white wine
    Fresh parsley
    1 lb. spaghetti, cooked, rinsed in cool water, and drained

In a medium-mixing bowl beat or whisk the eggs and cream together. Stir in the Parmesan and set aside. In a large skillet, over medium heat, melt the butter and olive oil. Sauté the garlic for about a minute. Add the bacon and cook until crisp. Remove from pan, set aside and discard fat in pan. Then over medium heat, add wine, stirring until it evaporates. Add pasta and toss until well coated. Pour in egg mixture and stir until eggs are cooked and fluffy, about 5 minutes. Serve immediately, topped with a sprig of parsley.

Serves 5-6

ASPARAGUS, MUSHROOM AND PARMESAN OMELET

Here's a tip: an omelet pan saves the hassle of folding the omelet over and produces a beautiful, perfect omelet every time.

> 3 large eggs
> 2 Tbs. milk
> 2 Tbs. olive oil
> 1/2 cup canned asparagus pieces
> 1/2 cup fresh mushrooms, sliced
> Salt and pepper to taste
> 1/2 cup Parmesan or Mozzarella cheese, grated

In a small mixing bowl, beat the eggs and milk until frothy. In a small non-stick pan, heat the olive oil over low heat and add the egg mixture. As the eggs cook, tilt the pan slightly so that the uncooked eggs reach the bottom of the pan. When the eggs have barely set, add the asparagus and mushrooms in the center. Season with salt and pepper. Add cheese. Gently fold over with a spatula and hold until the two sides are together. Carefully flip over and heat the other side of the omelet. Turn out onto a warm plate and serve immediately.

Serves 1

QUICHE SICILIAN STYLE

Planning a brunch? Make this quiche ahead and reheat it just before guests arrive.

> 2 Tbs. olive oil
> 1/2 small red onion, diced
> 1/2 cup small broccoli florets
> 2 Roma tomatoes, diced
> 4 large eggs
> 1 1/2 cups heavy cream
> Salt and pepper to taste
> 1/4 cup fresh basil, chopped
> 1/2 cup Mozzarella cheese
> 1/4 cup canned black olives, pitted and sliced
> Italian parsley
> 1/4 tsp. of dried Italian seasoning
> 1 9-inch frozen, unbaked piecrust

Heat oven to 325 degrees. In a large skillet, heat oil over medium heat and sauté onion and broccoli for 3 to 4 minutes. Add tomatoes, cook 1 minute, and remove from heat. In a large mixing bowl, beat eggs and cream and season with salt and pepper. Gently fold in basil, Italian seasoning and sautéed vegetables. Stir in cheese and olives. Pour mixture into piecrust. Place quiche on a baking sheet to prevent spillage and bake for 25 to 30 minutes or until a toothpick tests clean in the center. Cool quiche for 5 minutes before cutting into slicing. Serve topped with Italian parsley.

Serves 4-6

HEARTY BREAKFAST FRITTATA

Flat omelets are frittatas to Italians. They're easier to prepare than omelets and can make leftovers a real treat.

> Extra-virgin olive oil
> 1 large green bell pepper, diced
> 1 large red bell pepper, diced
> 1 small yellow onion, diced
> 2 potatoes, peeled and diced
> Salt and black pepper
> 3 large eggs
> 2 Tbs. milk
> 2 Tbs. Parmesan cheese
> 1/2 cup cured black olives
> Italian parsley

In a non-stick medium skillet, heat oil, peppers, onion and potatoes over medium heat. Cook until tender, about 15 minutes, stirring often. Season with salt and black pepper to taste. In a medium sized bowl, beat together eggs and milk, mixing well. Stir in cheese, then pour mixture over vegetables and olives. Reduce heat, cover pan and cook until eggs are set and no longer runny, about 5 minutes. Place a warm dish over pan, and invert pan so that the frittata will turn out perfectly upside down on the dish. Serve topped with a sprig of Italian parsley.

Serves 4

RICOTTA PANCAKES

In a large mixing bowl, mix 6 servings of your favorite pancake flour, with 1 cup ricotta cheese. Follow the box directions and spoon batter onto a lightly greased griddle or skillet. Cook and flip pancakes until both sides are golden. Serve with warm maple syrup, butter and a big bowl of fresh fruit alongside.

Serves 6

ITALIAN FRENCH TOAST

Move over France! Rich Italian Panettone, an egg bread full of fruit, is a magnificent way to make the classic fried toast. Serve this with fresh Italian sausage and a bowl of seasonal fruit.

    2 large eggs
    1/3 cup milk
    1/2 tsp. almond extract
    1 package sugar substitute
    4 thick slices of Italian Panettone
    2 Tbs. butter

In a shallow mixing bowl, stir together eggs, milk, almond extract, and sugar substitute. Dip the slices of bread into the egg mixtures on both sides. In a non-stick skillet, heat the butter over medium heat and fry the egg-soaked bread until golden brown on each side, about 10-12 minutes. Cover with foil to keep warm until serving.

Serves 2

RICOTTA CRESPELLE

Crespelle are thin Italian-style crepes. They can be prepared and held in a baking dish until ready to serve. Momma May always serves them with warm blueberry syrup, topped with fresh blueberries. A non-stick crepe pan works best here.

Crespelle batter:
> 1 cup flour
> 4 eggs
> 1 cup milk
> 1 Tbs. sugar
> 1/8 tsp. salt
> 1/2 cup water
> 4 Tbs. butter, melted

Filling:
> 1 cup ricotta cheese
> 1/2 cup golden raisins
> 1 Tbs. orange zest
> 2 Tbs. sugar
> 1/2 cup powdered sugar

Topping:
> Blueberry syrup, warmed
> Fresh blueberries

In a large bowl, blend all pancake ingredients except the butter. Cover and refrigerate for 1 hour.

Heat a crepe pan over medium heat. Brush with butter and spoon about 3 tablespoons crepe mixture in pan and swirl to coat evenly. Cook until the surface is golden brown and slightly dry. Loosen the edges, remove and cool. Stack crespelle between layers of wax paper or parchment.

In a large bowl, mix all filling ingredients together except powdered sugar. Spread over half of crepe. Fold crepe ends into middle. Place on serving platter and serve sprinkled with powdered sugar. Serve with warm blueberry syrup and fresh blueberries.

Serves 6

RASPBERRY FRUTTA SAUCE

Spoon this warm, sumptuous fruit sauce over pound cake, or Italian ice in the summertime.

> 2 pints fresh raspberries
> 1 1/4 cups light brown sugar
> 1/2 cup Amaretto
> 2 Tbs. honey
> 1 tsp. vanilla extract
> 2 Tbs. butter
> 1 cup almond biscotti cookies, crumbled

Heat oven to 350 degrees. Place raspberries in an ungreased baking dish. Mix all ingredients, except the butter and cookie crumbles. Pour over fruit. Cover top with pats of butter. Bake, uncovered, for 15 minutes or until hot and bubbly. Stir gently to loosen the sugar. Stir in the cookie crumbles. Serve warm over pound cake.

Serves 6

STRAWBERRIES WITH SABAYONE

Serve this custardy sauce in your best goblets over the most delicious berries you can find.

   2 pints fresh strawberries, washed and stemmed
   2 cups Marsala wine
   1 cup sugar
   6 egg yolks
   1/2 cup heavy cream, whipped
   2 Tbs. brown sugar

Place berries in a shallow serving dish and pour 1 cup of wine over them. Pour a small amount of water into a double boiler and heat water until it is just warm. Beat sugar and egg yolks in the top of the double boiler until yellow and thick. Place over double boiler. Gradually beat remaining cup of wine into the eggs and cook, whisking constantly, until thick. Careful! Never bring the mixture to a boil. Place strawberries in goblets, and pour warm sauce over them. Top with dollops of cream and sprinkle with brown sugar.

Serves 6

ITALIAN FRUIT SALAD

Besides being a fine fruit salad, this makes an easy and refreshing topping for ice cream, cake or sorbet.

   2 large navel oranges
   2 apples
   1 kiwi
   2 peaches
   1 pint strawberries or black berries
   1/2 cup Amaretto
   1 cup Asti Spumante or sparkling apple juice
   2 Tbs. fresh lemon juice
   2 Tbs. sugar

Cut all fruit into bite-sized chunks and place in a large bowl. Stir in remaining ingredients, cover, and chill for 1 hour.

Serves 6

AUNT SARA'S SAVORY ORANGE SALAD

Serve this quick salad with a loaf of crusty bread to soak up the salty, sweet juices.

> 4 large navel or blood oranges
> 1 Tbs. olive oil
> 1 Tbs. wine vinegar
> Salt and pepper to taste

Peel and remove all white membrane from the oranges. Section the fruit, then cut pieces in half. Combine remaining ingredients and pour over oranges. Cover and chill for about 30 minutes.

Serves 4

POTATO CHEESE BALLS

We serve these Sicilian version of croquettes as finger food or piled on a platter at brunchtime.

2 lbs. medium baking potatoes, peeled and quartered
2 Tbs. butter
2 Tbs. fresh parsley, chopped
1/2 cup Pecorino or Mozzarella cheese, grated
1 1/2 cups Italian bread crumbs
Salt and pepper to taste
2 large eggs, separated
Olive oil

Boil potatoes in lightly salted water to cover until tender, about 20 minutes. Drain and mash potatoes. Mix in butter, parsley, cheese and 1/2 cup of crumbs. Season with salt and pepper. Stir in egg yolks.

In a medium bowl, lightly beat egg whites until frothy and set aside. Place remaining crumbs in another small bowl and set aside.

Form small 1-inch balls with the potato mixture; dip them first into the egg white then roll in crumbs, moistening your hands with water, as needed, to keep mixture from sticking. Roll the balls in your hand, pressing in the crumbs thoroughly. In a large skillet over medium heat, heat enough olive oil to partially cover the balls. Fry them until golden brown. Drain balls on paper towels and serve hot.

Serves 8-10

MONTE CRISTO ITALIANO

Serve these great gooey sandwiches plain, or dusted with powdered sugar, and a bowl of homemade jam.

> 1 loaf Italian bread, unsliced
> 8 ozs. Mozzarella cheese, thinly sliced
> 2 eggs
> 1/2 cup milk
> 1 Tbs. vanilla
> 1 cup flour
> Peanut or sunflower oil for deep-frying
> 1/2 cup powdered sugar

Slice bread into eight pieces, remove crusts, and make cheese sandwiches. Cut each in half diagonally, forming triangles. Beat the eggs, milk and vanilla together and set aside. Place flour in a large shallow dish. Dip the sandwiches into eggs, then lightly dredge in flour. Repeat with remaining eggs and flour.

In a large skillet, heat enough oil over medium high to almost cover the sandwiches. When the oil is very hot but not smoking, fry the sandwiches until golden on both sides. Drain them on paper towels and place on a large serving platter. Serve sprinkled with powdered sugar.

Serves 6-8

CRACKED PEPPER FOCACCIA

Focaccia, or "hearth," bread began centuries before the modern oven appeared. Large flat rounds of dough were cooked directly on hot stones to create a cross between pizza and bread as we know it today.

1 Tbs. active dry or quick rising yeast
1 tsp. sugar
2 cups lukewarm water, (about 85-95 degrees)
6 Tbs. extra-virgin olive oil
1 Tbs. cracked black pepper
2 tsps. salt
4 3/4 cups white flour
1 1/2 tsps. dried thyme
2 Tbs. dried rosemary, crushed
2 tsps. coarse sea salt

In a large bowl, dissolve yeast and sugar in water. Stir in 5 tablespoons olive oil, pepper and salt. Add 1 cup flour and stir vigorously with a wooden spoon until flour is well incorporated. Beat in enough remaining flour, about 1/2 cup at a time, to form a dough that is soft and sticky but not completely smooth. Oil a large bowl. Scrape dough into bowl and cover with plastic wrap. Let dough rise in warm, draft free area until doubled in volume, about 45 minutes.

Lightly oil a 15-inch x 10-inch x 1-inch baking sheet. Do not deflate dough. Slide it onto prepared baking sheet. Dough will be soft and should slide easily onto pan. Gently pull and stretch dough so that it almost covers baking sheet. Press fingertips all over top of dough to form indentations. Brush top of focaccia with remaining olive oil. Sprinkle with spices and salt and let rise for 15 min. in draft free area.

Heat oven to 450 degrees. Bake focaccia on center oven rack for 15-20 or until golden brown.

Makes 1 large flatbread

CHAPTER 7

EVERYONE'S ITALIAN-PASTA & MORE

In a Sicilian household, pasta is present at nearly every meal. If you, too, are a serious noodle lover, read these few tips before setting the water on to boil.

Always buy a premium imported Italian brand of frozen or dried pasta. Use the biggest pot you have, allowing 6 quarts of lightly salted water per pound of pasta. The water has got to be at a convincing boil. Otherwise you'll have soggy mush. Cook, stirring often, until the noodles are just tender. Then drain and mix them with the sauce. If you decide to use frozen pasta, don't thaw it before cooking or the strands or shapes will stick to one another.

Before dropping the pasta into a pot of boiling water, have a large colander at the ready. Be sure that whatever sauce you've chosen is well underway or finished. As soon as the noodles are done, mix them thoroughly with the sauce. Nothing sits on top of the pasta when it comes to the Sicilian table.

Is it pasta yet? Just how long do you cook noodles? Al dente-- what is it exactly? Each time you cook pasta, taste it when it appears to be almost done. It should be just tender but firm to the bite. By all means don't rely on package instructions!

Which pasta? Which sauce? There are over 600 pasta shapes so forget focusing on them! Instead concentrate on the consistency and texture of the sauce and how it will stick to the pasta. A good rule of thumb is to choose more fluid sauces for long straight noodles and chunkier ones for the smaller fatter tubes and shapes. Count on 2 1/2 ounces of pasta per person as a first course and 4 ounces as an entrée.

Popular Pasta Shapes:

Capellini - Angel Hair
Fettuccine - Long, flat and wide
Fusilli - Corkscrews
Gnocchi - Potato dumplings
Lasagne - Long, flat very wide noodles
Linguine - Flat spaghetti
Orzo - Rice shaped
Penne - Thin tubes
Ravioli - Stuffed squares or circles
Rigatoni - Ridged large tubes
Spaghetti - Thin strands
Spaghettini - Thinner strands of spaghetti
Tortellini - Tiny stuffed pillows
Ziti - Medium tubes known as "bridegrooms" in Sicily

HOME MADE PASTA & RAVIOLI

When time allows, give yourself the joy of making fresh, soft, silky noodles.

>   2 cups all-purpose flour
>   1/2 tsp. salt
>   3 eggs
>   Additional flour for dusting
>   Water as needed

In a large bowl or on a flat surface, mix together flour and salt. Make a well in the center of the bowl and add eggs. Beat the eggs with a fork and gradually incorporate the flour. Mix in enough flour with your hands to make a rough dough. If dough is too sticky add a little flour; if the dough is too dry add a little water. Knead dough on a lightly floured surface until smooth and forms a ball. Cover with a wet towel and let rest for 10 minutes. Divide the dough into 4 sections. Work with one of the sections at a time, keeping the other remaining sections wrapped tightly. At this point, you can either roll out the dough by hand or use a pasta machine. Both give good results.

Hand Rolled Pasta: Roll one section of the dough out on a lightly floured surface. Sprinkle each side of dough with a little flour. With a rolling pin, roll the dough out to a 1/8-inch thick rectangle. Lightly sprinkle with flour and fold into thirds lengthwise, slightly over the center. Bring remaining side over folded dough, as if folding a letter. Cut crosswise into desired width. For example: linguine should be cut 1/8" thick; fettuccine 1/4" thick, etc. Place finished pasta on a clean dishtowel and sprinkle with flour. Repeat with remaining dough.

Cook pasta immediately or freeze it for up to 4 months by placing in freezer bags or an airtight container.

Using a Pasta Machine: Set the pasta machine on the widest setting. Flatten one part of the dough on a floured surface with your hands, and then feed the lightly floured dough through the rollers. Place the rolled strip flat on the table and fold in half. Repeat until dough is soft and easily fits through slot. If dough sticks to machine, lightly dust both sides with flour. When dough is ready to be rolled, feed it through progressively narrower settings until it is 1/8-inch thick. Then, feed dough through cutting rollers for desired shape. Placed finished pasta on a clean dishtowel and sprinkle with flour. Cook immediately or freeze for up to 4 months by placing in freezer bags or an airtight container.

Serves 4 as an appetizer or side dish

Fresh Ravioli: Roll the dough through the machine on the second thinnest setting. Cut the dough sheets into 20-inch lengths. Cover the dough in plastic wrap to keep it soft until ready to shape. Fold each sheet in half to form a crease down the center that will be the guide. Place a spoonful of mixture in 2 rows along opposite sides. Lightly brush a little water around the sides and lay the second sheet of pasta over the top to cover the filling. With your fingers, gently press down around each mound sealing the dough. Using a pastry wheel, cut into squares around each mound. Place each square upside down on a clean dishtowel and lightly dust with flour.
To Cook Ravioli: Place in lightly salted boiling water. When ravioli float to the top, after 5-6 minutes, remove with a slotted spoon to a serving bowl.

PASTA SAUCES

The essential herbs used in Italian cooking are basil, parsley, oregano, and garlic. You just can't cook Italian without 'em!

Good quality canned plum tomatoes are better than out-of-season fresh ones, especially for pasta sauces. If you do choose fresh tomatoes be sure that they are firm and red and packed with flavor. Plum tomatoes are ideal for pasta because their flesh is thick and meaty. In any case, choose ripeness and flavor. Here's a small tip. Never refrigerate a tomato or the flavor will diminish rapidly. Slightly underripe tomatoes left on a warm windowsill will ripen quickly.

Fresh Raw Tomato Sauce

Sugar will help balance the acidity in this sauce. Serve this one with freshly grated Parmesan cheese.

> 6-7 ripe tomatoes, seeded and diced
> 1 garlic clove, minced
> 1/2 tsp. sugar
> 5 Tbs. extra virgin olive oil
> 5-6 fresh basil leaves
> Salt and pepper to taste

In a medium-sized bowl, mix together tomatoes, garlic, sugar, oil and basil. Season with salt and pepper to taste. Set aside while pasta cooks to let the flavors blend together. Toss with linguine, straight or ziti pasta.

Makes enough for 1 pound of pasta

Clam Sauce

This quick sauce is not only tasty but low in calories.

> 1-4 garlic cloves, chopped
> 2 Tbs. butter
> 1 Tbs. olive oil
> 1 2-oz. can clams, finely chopped with juice reserved
> 6 sprigs Italian parsley, minced
> 1 tsp. red pepper flakes
> 1/2 tsp. black pepper

In a medium non stick skillet, sauté garlic in butter and olive oil for 2 minutes. Add clam juice and parsley. Mix in clams and red pepper flakes. Season with black pepper and remove when clams are warm. Do not overcook clams or they will be tough. Serve over linguine.

Makes enough for 1 pound of pasta

Lemon Sauce

The tangy lemon cuts the heaviness of a regular rich, creamy sauce.

> 2 tsps. fresh lemon zest
> 10 oz. butter
> 1/4 cup dry white wine
> Cayenne pepper to taste
> 2 cups heavy cream
> 2 Tbs. lemon juice
> Salt and pepper

In a medium skillet, heat lemon zest in the butter over very low heat. After 1 minute add wine, cream and cayenne. Simmer for 3-5 minutes, then remove from heat. Stir in lemon juice and season with salt and pepper. Stir and toss with egg noodle pasta or lobster filled ravioli.

Makes enough for 1 pound of pasta

Seafood Sauce

A fisherman's tasty delight!

> 6 oz. butter
> 1/4 cup olive oil
> 1/2 sweet red pepper, sliced thin
> 2 garlic cloves, minced
> 2 shallots, chopped
> 1/2 lb. medium shrimp
> 1/4 lb. crabmeat
> 1/4 lb. scallops
> Juice of 1 medium lemon
> 1/2 cup white wine

In a large skillet, melt butter and oil over medium heat. Add pepper, garlic and shallots and sauté for 2-3 minutes. Mix in seafood and sauté until fully cooked, about 6-8 minutes. Stir in lemon juice and wine. Simmer 2-3 minutes. Serve over fettuccine, tortellini or gnocchi.

Makes enough for 1 pound of pasta

Garlic and Oil Sauce   Aglio e Olio

Be careful not to cook the garlic too quickly. It can easily burn and become bitter.

1/2 cup olive oil
Crushed red pepper to taste
2 garlic cloves, minced
Salt and black pepper to taste

In a medium skillet, heat olive oil over low heat. Add hot pepper and garlic. Cook slowly, until golden brown, about 5-7 minutes. Season with salt and pepper. Serve with straight or string cut pastas or any stuffed variety of tortellini.

Makes enough for 1 pound of pasta

Pesto Sauce

Toss this classic sauce over straight cuts of pasta.

1 cup fresh basil
1/2 cup Parmesan cheese, grated
1/2 cup pine nuts, toasted
1/2 cup fresh Italian parsley
3-4 garlic cloves
1/2 cup extra-virgin olive oil
1 tsp. salt
1/2 tsp. pepper

Place all ingredients in a blender or food processor and blend until smooth. Use immediately, or refrigerate.

Makes enough for 1 pound of pasta

Carbonara Sauce

A generous amount of chopped parsley, grated cheese and freshly ground black pepper will add the final touch to this sauce.

>   3 large garlic cloves, crushed
>   1 Tbs. olive oil
>   2 Tbs. unsalted butter
>   1/4 cup dry white wine
>   1/2 lb. bacon, diced
>   3 eggs plus 2 yolks
>   2 Tbs. milk or heavy cream (optional)
>   Freshly ground black pepper
>   3/4 cup Parmesan cheese, freshly grated
>   1/2 tsp. salt
>   3 Tbs. Italian parsley, chopped

In a large skillet over medium low heat, sauté garlic, oil and butter until the garlic begins to color. Stir in wine and simmer for 2 minutes. Remove from heat and discard garlic. In a separate pan, sauté the bacon until it is brown, but not crisp. Drain all but 2 tablespoons of fat, and add to skillet. In a medium-sized bowl, blend the egg yolks and eggs with the remainder of the ingredients except parsley. Just before pasta is ready, reheat the sauce. Drain cooked pasta and place in hot pan. Mix to coat thoroughly with the sauce. Then stir in egg mixture and cook 1-2 minutes or until egg is cooked. Serve with any straight or string cut pastas.

Makes enough for 1 pound of pasta

Bolognese Sauce

This is a good sauce to make when you're using a chunky tube shaped noodle. Serve with freshly grated Parmesan cheese.

2 Tbs. olive oil
2 Tbs. butter
1 carrot, finely chopped
1 small onion, finely chopped
1/2 lb. lean ground beef
1/2 lb. Italian sausage meat
1 garlic clove, finely chopped
1 celery stalk, finely chopped
1 bay leaf
3 28 oz. cans Italian-style tomatoes, drained and chopped
2/3 cup red wine
1 tsp. salt
1/2 tsp. pepper

In a large skillet or saucepan, melt oil and butter over medium heat. Add carrots and onions and cook for 10 minutes, stirring occasionally, until carrots are tender. Stir in beef and sausage

and cook until meat is no longer pink. Drain fat. Stir in remaining ingredients. Heat to boiling then reduce to low, cover and simmer for about 45 minutes.

Makes enough for 1 pound of pasta

Prosciutto, Peas and Asparagus Sauce

Try this one over straight pasta or tortellini and don't forget the freshly grated cheese!

> 4 oz. prosciutto, chopped
> 2 bunches of green onions, thinly sliced
> 4 Tbs. extra-virgin olive oil
> 2 lbs. asparagus, tough stalks removed and tips sliced
> 1 1/2 cups shelled peas
> diagonally, about 1 inch long
> Salt and pepper

In a medium skillet, sauté prosciutto and onions in oil until onions are translucent, about 5 minutes. Add the asparagus, peas and 1/2 cup water. Cook for about 20 minutes, or until asparagus are quite tender. Season with salt and pepper to taste.

Makes enough for 1 pound of pasta

Cheese Ravioli Filling

> 8 oz. ricotta cheese
> 1 cup fresh basil, chopped
> 1 cup fresh parsley, chopped
> 2 eggs
> 1/2 cup Parmesan cheese, grated
> 1 tsp. nutmeg
> 1/4 tsp. salt
> 1/2 tsp. pepper

In a large bowl, combine all ingredients and stir until completely mixed. Place by spoonfuls onto dough.

Makes enough filling for about 4 dozen medium raviolis

WINNING PASTA COMBOS

TRADITIONAL SPAGHETTI SAUCE AND MEATBALLS

Without the meatballs, this makes a prize winning vegetarian sauce. If possible, use Heinz or Hunts tomato sauce and Progresso breadcrumbs. For the best meatballs, use meat that is labeled 80/20%. This refers to the lean versus fat content of the meat. This makes enough for a small army so freeze a good portion in empty milk containers if you have them.

For the red sauce:
    2 large onions, finely minced
    4 Tbs. garlic, chopped
    6 Tbs. olive oil
    2 #10 cans tomato sauce
    2 #10 cans or 48 ozs. tomato paste
    2 #10 cans water
    1 Tbs. crushed red pepper flakes
    1/2 tsp. ground cloves
    2 Tbs. dried sweet basil
    3 Tbs. salt
    1/2 cup sugar

In a large soup pot, sauté onions and garlic in oil over medium high heat until brown, about 12-15 minutes. Add all remaining ingredients and simmer for 1 hour and 15 minutes. Add browned meatballs and simmer for an additional 45 minutes.

For the meatballs:

4 pounds lean hamburger
4 Tbs. garlic, minced
4 Tbs. dried parsley
4 Tbs. Parmesan cheese, grated
5 eggs
2 Tbs. salt
1/2 Tbs. pepper
15 oz. Italian-style breadcrumbs
1 cup water

In a large bowl, mix all ingredients until well combined. Form egg-shaped meatballs, approx. 2 1/2 oz. each. Film a large sauté pan with olive oil and brown meatballs. The inside of the meatball will not be fully cooked.

Makes 2 gallons sauce and 30 meatballs

SPAGHETTI WITH TOASTED BREAD CRUMBS

This is one of those pasta dishes best served without cheese! Season generously with freshly cracked pepper.

1/4 cup extra-virgin olive oil
1/4 cup fresh homemade breadcrumbs
Salt and pepper to taste
1 tsp. sugar
1/2 cup or about 2 bunches Italian parsley, chopped
1 lb. spaghetti

Bring 6 quarts water to boil in a large spaghetti pot with 2 tablespoons salt.

In a 12-inch sauté pan, heat olive oil over low heat. Add bread-crumbs, salt and pepper and sugar. Cook, stirring constantly, until golden brown, about 3 to 4 minutes. Remove from heat, stir in parsley, and set aside. Cook spaghetti until just tender. Drain and pour into sauté pan. Toss pasta over medium heat to thoroughly coat with sauce. Serve immediately.

Serves 4

FETTUCCINE ALFREDO

Although Alfredo sauce hails from Roma, it's still a favorite of our entire Sicilian family.

> 12 ozs. fettuccine, fresh or dried
> 1 cup evaporated skimmed milk
> 1/2 cup nonfat sour cream
> 1 cup Parmesan cheese, grated
> 2 Tbs. butter
> Freshly ground pepper

In a large pasta pot, bring 3 quarts of lightly salted water to a boil and cover the pot. Heat the water to boiling over high heat. Add the fettuccine and cook until just tender. As the pasta cooks, heat the milk in a medium saucepan. Remove from heat and stir in sour cream and cheese. Add butter and stir until it melts. The sauce will thicken slightly. When pasta is cooked, drain and return it to the pasta pot. Pour in sauce and toss to thoroughly coat pasta. Season generously with pep-per. Toss again and serve with additional grated Parmesan.

Serves 4

PUTTANESCA

The name of this sauce comes from puttana or prostitute. It's cooked quickly and in the old days could be made and sometimes eaten in between customers. Even today in Italy you can occasionally see 'ladies of the night' building their fires and making a quick snack when there's time.

> 1 lb. spaghetti
> 4 Tbs. olive oil
> 1 tsp. crushed red pepper flakes
> 2 garlic cloves, minced
> 2 anchovy filets, chopped
> 2 lbs. fresh chopped tomatoes, peeled and seeded
> 1 tsp. sugar
> 1/4 cup fresh Italian parsley, chopped
> 1/2 cup black Italian olives, pitted
> 1 Tbs. capers
> Parmesan cheese, grated

Cook pasta in boiling water, until just tender. Make the sauce as the pasta cooks. In a large skillet, heat oil over medium high and sauté red pepper flakes, garlic and anchovies. Cook, stirring constantly, until anchovies have melted. Raise heat to high and add tomatoes, sugar and parsley. Cook until thickened, about 15 minutes. Add olives and capers. When pasta has cooked, drain, and toss with sauce. Serve immediately topped with Parmesan cheese.

Serves 4

CLASSIC LASAGNE

Make this soul-satisfying dish when you have a crowd to feed. If you don't have any homemade pasta sauce at hand, use the best quality commercial one you can find.

1-15 oz. container Ricotta cheese
1/2 cup Parmesan cheese, grated
2 eggs
4-5 cups spaghetti sauce, (see pg. 125)
1 lb. dry no-boil lasagne noodles
1 lb. lean ground beef, cooked and drained
4 cups Mozzarella cheese, shredded
1 Tbs. parsley, finely chopped

Preheat oven to 350 degrees. In a large bowl, mix together ricotta, Parmesan, and eggs. Lightly grease a 1-inch x 9-inch baking dish. Spread 1 cup spaghetti sauce on the bottom. Make three consecutive layers of noodles, cheese mixture, meat sauce and mozzarella, ending with mozzarella. Top with parsley. Cover tightly and bake 1 hour or until hot and bubbly. Let stand covered for 15 minutes before serving.

ZITI AL FORNO

Adding a little starchy pasta water to the sauce is a great way to give sauces a silken, smooth consistency. Any tube pasta like penne or rigatoni and be substituted for the ziti.

3 Tbs. extra-virgin olive oil
4 garlic cloves, minced
2 14 oz. cans Italian plum tomatoes
1 tsp. dried oregano
1 tsp. dried basil
1 tsp. sugar
1 lb. ziti pasta
8 oz. Mozzarella cheese, shredded
1 cup Parmesan cheese, grated
Salt and pepper to taste

Preheat oven to 375 degrees. In a large skillet, heat oil and garlic over medium heat until garlic is translucent, about 3-5 minutes. Add tomatoes, oregano, basil and sugar, and simmer for about 20 minutes or slightly thick. Season with salt and pepper. Bring a large pot of salted water to the boil and cook ziti until just tender or 'al dente,' reserving 1/2 cup of pasta water. Set aside. Reserve 1/2 cup of the sauce. Toss pasta in remaining sauce and add reserved pasta water a little at a time. Place half the pasta in a glass baking dish 12-inch x 10-inch and sprinkle 1/2 of both cheeses over top. Cover with remaining sauce, spreading evenly. Sprinkle with the remaining cheese. Bake, uncovered, for about 20 minutes or until bubbly and golden brown.

Serves 4

SICILIAN EGGPLANT AND PASTA

This healthy and full-bodied dish is a one-pot meal, needing only a simple salad to go with it.

> 1 cup olive oil
> 2 garlic cloves, minced
> 1 large eggplant, about 1 pound, cut into 1-inch cubes, salted and drained
> 1/4 tsp. fresh ground black pepper
> 1/2 cup tomato paste
> 2 Tbs. water
> 1 tsp. dried oregano
> 1/2 cup Kalamata or Greek olives, pitted and sliced
> 2 Tbs. capers
> 3/4 lb. ziti pasta
> 1/2 cup Parmesan cheese, grated
> 5-6 fresh basil leaves, chopped

In a large skillet, heat oil and add garlic, eggplant and pepper. Cook over medium heat for about 10 minutes. Reduce heat to low and add tomato paste, water, oregano, olives and capers. Simmer until eggplant is soft, about 15-20 minutes. Stir often to prevent eggplant from sticking. Meanwhile cook pasta in a large pot of salted boiling water until just tender. When cooked, drain, then add to eggplant sauce and toss until well coated. Serve topped with Parmesan and basil.

Serves 4

ANGEL HAIR PASTA AND GARLIC

Capellini cook fast. You'll find them quickly floating to the top of the pot. Be careful not to overdo it!

> 1 lb. capellini or angel hair pasta
> 1/2 cup extra-virgin olive oil
> 1/4 cup fresh Italian parsley, chopped
> 1/4 cup fresh basil, chopped
> 4-5 garlic cloves, finely chopped
> Parmesan cheese, freshly grated
> Freshly ground black pepper

In a large pot of lightly salted boiling water, cook pasta until just tender. Make the sauce just before or as pasta cooks. In a large skillet over medium heat, heat oil and sauté parsley, basil and garlic, stirring often, until garlic is soft, about 3-5 minutes. When pasta is cooked, drain and immediately add to skillet.

Toss gently until coated. Serve topped with cheese and freshly grated black pepper.

Serves 4

GNOCCHI

Not technically a pasta, these little handmade potato dumplings make a hearty but elegant first course.

> 1 lb. potatoes, peeled and quartered
> 1 egg, beaten
> 1/2 cup Parmesan cheese, grated
> 1/4 tsp. each salt and nutmeg
> 1 cup semolina or all-purpose flour
> 2 1/2 cups spaghetti sauce, heated
> 1 Tbs. fresh parsley, finely chopped

In a large pot, boil the potatoes in lightly salted water for 15 minutes or until tender. Drain and cool. Mash the potatoes then beat in the egg, cheese, salt and nutmeg, mixing thoroughly. Add flour very gradually, blending until a stiff dough forms. Form a ball with the dough, and then roll onto a lightly floured surface forming a long cylinder. Cut 1/2-inch pieces of dough, and make a small dent in each piece with your finger. Place finished gnocchi on a floured board until ready to cook, or put into zip-lock bags and freeze.

In a large saucepan, bring lightly salted water to boil. Drop gnocchi in pot and cook about 10 minutes or until they rise to the surface. Remove with a slotted spoon.

Place in a bowl and toss with spaghetti sauce. Serve topped with Parmesan cheese and parsley.

Serves 4

CHAPTER 8

BREAD, WINE, CHEESE, OLIVES and HERBS
SIMPLE FOODS TO SAVOR

BREAD

As the world is merely earth, water, fire and air, bread, too, is just flour, water, yeast and salt. Four elemental ingredients– grain from the earth, water from the ocean, salt from the embers of the sea, and leavening from the air. It celebrates the simplest and most primal pleasures.

Life without bread in Sicily is simply inconceivable. In fact, all over Italy we are known for a variety of rough country loaves with thick chewy crusts, bread sticks, thin and fat, short and long. We've got rolls imaginatively coiled, twisted and slashed, as well as so many varieties of flat breads. Focaccia can be found with wild herbs or filled with candied fruit, grapes and nuts. Bread to taste the olive oil, bread to sip with espresso, bread to dip in Marsala. It is the backbone of each meal.

"Grace is available for each of us every day--our spiritual daily bread-- but we've got to remember to ask for it with a grateful heart and and not worry about whether there will be enough for tomorrow."--Sarah Ban Breathnack

STEPS TO BAKING THE BEST BREAD

DISSOLVING YEAST:

Almost every leavened bread recipe begins by dissolving yeast in a small amount of warm water. Use packets of rapid rise dry yeast for best results, stirring in the granules with a whisk. Don't use yeast that has passed its expiration date; check each time before opening the packet.

MIXING THE DOUGH:

It is not necessary to sift flour. We've debated this for years, but I personally find flour sifting a waste of time that produces no better results in bread.

BY HAND:

Mama May taught us that mixing dough by hand produces a far lighter and better tasting bread because it allows more air bubbles to remain in the dough.

Pour the flour into a pile on a flat surface or counter. Make a well in the center and pour in the liquid. Gradually incorporate flour from the sides into the middle with your hands and mix together until well blended. It will be quite sticky at first so have a bottle of olive oil handy to moisten your hands with. This helps to remove the dough from your fingers and adds a little extra zip to the bread. The softer the dough, the lighter it will be after baking. So look for a soft but not too sticky mixture. After kneading the dough, form a ball and brush it with olive oil. Place it in a large, deep bowl and cover with a damp cloth.

BY MIXER:

I prefer to use Kitchen Aid mixer. The hook attachment quickly and easily mixes bread dough. After dissolving the yeast in warm water in a small separate bowl, pour the flour into the mixer. Slowly add the yeast mixture along with any other ingredients and mix until well blended. Remove the dough, lightly coat with olive oil, form into a ball and place in a deep bowl to rise.

KNEADING:

The warmth of your hand along with gentle yet firm "punching down" action produces the best results. Mama May never allowed Dad to knead the dough. She felt that his hands were too big and that he was too rough on dough. Be careful! Pour a small amount of olive oil on your hands, then make a fist to punch down the dough, using a circular motion. Continue this action until the dough has thoroughly deflated. It should be soft and elastic. Don't over knead the dough! All of this can be done in the big bowl. Once it has deflated, form another ball.

RISING:

All yeast breads need to rise twice. Patience! Use a large enough bowl or pan that allows the bread to double or triple in size. Always keep the dough in a warm area and cover the top of the pan with a dish towel, then a blanket or heavy cloth. It's the old-fashioned and best way! In fact, some Italian women used to place the dough in a bed still warm from a sleeping body, pull the blanket up over the bowl, tucking in the corners, and let it rise.

BAKING:

You do not have to have a baking stone for crusty bread, although having one does help distribute the heat a little more evenly. Adding moisture or steam is what gives a crunchy crust. You can either place a broiler pan in the oven with about 1 1/2 cups of boiling water on the bottom shelf or use a mister and spray water in the oven during the first 10 minutes of baking.

BASIC BREAD DOUGH

In a large bowl, dissolve yeast and sugar in warm water. Let stand for about 10 minutes or until foamy. Mix together flour and salt on a large flat surface. Make a well in the center and pour in the yeast, oil and remaining water. Mix with your hands until flour has been absorbed. Add a little more warm water if necessary. Begin kneading dough, adding flour to the work surface to prevent sticking. If dough sticks to your hands, moisten them with olive oil. Knead the dough until it becomes very soft and elastic, about 10-12 minutes. Shape into a ball and place in a large, deep bowl. Cover with a kitchen towel and blanket and leave in a warm draft-free area to rise. When dough has doubled or tripled in size, punch it down gently with your fist and fold over several times. Shape into a ball again, cover and let rise. When dough has once again doubled in size, punch it down again, drizzle with a little more olive oil, and shape into a ball. Place it in an oiled bread pan or onto a baking stone. Preheat oven to 375 degrees and bake 25-30 minutes or until golden brown. Cool on a wire rack.

Makes 1 large loaf

PEPPERONI BREAD

Years ago, bread, along with a liter of wine, was actually the Italian peasant worker's salary. A man that is down to earth and has a heart of gold is a man 'buono come il pane' or good like bread. We'd just say as 'good as gold.'

> 1 packet rapid rise yeast
> 3/4 cup lukewarm water
> 1 Tbs. salt
> 2 Tbs. sugar
> 2 Tbs. olive oil
> 2 1/2 lbs. all-purpose flour
> 1 cup pepperoni, thinly sliced
> 1 cup Mozzarella cheese, shredded
> Sesame seeds, optional

In a large mixing bowl, dissolve yeast in water and let stand for 10 minutes or until foamy. Stir in salt, sugar and oil. Beat in 1 cup flour thoroughly, then add another 1 1/2 cups flour. Knead using a mixer with a hook, 8-10 minutes or knead the dough by hand about 15 minutes until it is smooth and elastic, adding the rest of the flour as needed to prevent sticking. Place dough on a floured surface and knead until it is smooth and silky. Place in a very deep bowl, drizzle to coat with olive oil and cover. Let rise until doubled, about 1 1/2 hours. Punch down dough and let rise once more. Lightly oil a baking sheet. Punch it down again, turn onto a floured surface and divide dough in half. Roll each half into 12-inch flat log. Place pepperoni and cheese evenly into the middle of the dough, then roll each piece tightly into a long slender loaf, pinching the edges to seal. Place on an oiled sheet pan and cover with a dish towel. Place in a warm draft-free area until doubled in size. Preheat oven to 375 degrees. If desired, brush tops of loaves with olive oil and sprinkle with sesame seeds. Bake for 20-25 minutes or until golden brown. Cool on wire rack.

WHOLE WHEAT ITALIAN BREAD

Every day in Italy, more than 3,500 dedicated bakers rise early to bake their bread. A good percentage of them make this bread or a close variation.

> 1 packet rapid rise yeast
> 1 1/2 cups warm water
> 1 Tbs. sugar
> 1 Tbs. olive oil
> 1 tsp. salt
> 1 cup whole wheat flour
> 2 1/2-3 cups unbleached all purpose flour
> 1/2 cup wheat germ
> 1 tsp. cornstarch dissolved in 1/3 cup water

In a large bowl, dissolve yeast in warm water and let stand for 5 minutes until foamy. Stir in sugar, oil and salt. Mix in whole wheat and 1 1/2 cups unbleached flour. In an electric mixer with a hook attachment, beat dough until it is elastic, about 10 minutes. Stir in wheat germ and about 1 more cup unbleached flour to make a stiff dough. Turn out onto a floured surface and knead until dough is smooth and springy and develops small bubbles just under surface. Place in a greased bowl turning dough to coat top. Cover and let rise in a warm place until doubled, about 1 hour. Punch dough down again, and let rise once more. Punch it down again, then turn it out onto a floured surface. Divide dough in half and shape each half into a slender oval loaf about 12-inches long. Place on greased baking sheets or in loaf pans and cover. Let rise until doubled in size. In a small saucepan, heat cornstarch mixture to a boil, stirring until thick and clear. Brush loaves with warm cornstarch mixture. Using a floured razor blade or sharp knife, make a slash in the center of each loaf. Preheat oven to 375 degrees. Bake for 25-30 minutes or until browned. Cool on wire rack.

Makes 2 oval loaves

POM O DORI ROLLS

Be sure to prepare the filling ahead or as the dough is rising so you'll have it at the ready when the bread has risen.

Tomato filling:
>1 small onion, finely chopped
>1 medium tomato, peeled and chopped
>1 garlic clove, minced
>1 8-oz. can tomato sauce
>1 tsp. dried basil
>1/4 tsp. salt
>Dash pepper

For the rolls:
>1 packet rapid rise yeast
>1 1/3 cups warm water
>1 Tbs. sugar
>2 Tbs. olive oil
>1 tsp. salt
>3 1/2-4 cups unbleached all-purpose flour
>1/4 cup Parmesan cheese, grated

In a small saucepan mix together all ingredients for the filling. Heat to a simmer and cook for 10 minutes. Set aside to cool.

In a large bowl, dissolve yeast in warm water and let stand for 5 minutes or until foamy. Stir in sugar, oil and salt. Add 2 1/2 cups flour and mix well. In an electric mixer with a hook attachment, beat dough until it is elastic, about 15 minutes. Stir in 1 cup additional flour or enough to make stiff dough. Turn out onto a floured surface and knead until smooth and supple, about 25 minutes. Dough will develop small bubbles just under the surface.

Lightly grease a baking sheet. Divide into 12 smooth balls and place them 2-3 inches apart on the prepared sheet. Using floured fingers, make a deep indentation in the center of each and fill with a generous tablespoon of the tomato filling. Sprinkle each with 1 teaspoon cheese. Cover lightly and let rise until nearly doubled, about 20 minutes. Meanwhile, preheat oven to 375 degrees. Bake rolls for 25-30 minutes or until golden brown. Cool slightly on a wire rack.

Makes 1 dozen rolls.

SESAME BREAD STICKS

1 packet rapid rise yeast
3/4 cup warm water
1 Tbs. malt syrup
2 Tbs. olive oil
3 1/2-4 cups unbleached all-purpose flour
1 1/2 tsps. salt
1/2 cup cornmeal for sprinkling
Option: Top before baking with poppy or sesame seeds

In a large mixing bowl, stir together yeast, water and syrup and let stand for 5 minutes or until foamy. Stir in oil. Add flour and salt and stir to form a dough. Knead by hand on a lightly floured surface until smooth and elastic, about 10 minutes. Place dough on a floured surface and shape into a 1-inch x 4-inch rectangle. Lightly brush the top of the dough with oil. Cover with a clean towel and place in a warm spot. Let rise until doubled, about 30 minutes.

Preheat oven to 450 degrees. Sprinkle the dough with cornmeal before cutting and stretching. Lightly oil a baking sheet. Cut the dough crosswise into 4 equal sections. Cut each section again crosswise into 5 strips, each about 1-inch in width.

Shape and roll each piece between your hands to form a bread-stick. Place on prepared sheet. Bake for 20 minutes or until golden brown.

Makes 2 dozen breadsticks

BATTER BREADS

Batter breads do not require bread machines or kneading of any kind. Just stir together the ingredients, pour into pans and 'ecco'!

APRICOT PECAN LOAF

> 5 cups all purpose flour
> 2 packets active dry yeast
> 2 Tbs. sugar
> 2 tsp. cinnamon
> 1 tsp. salt
> 1/4 tsp. baking soda
> 1 1/2 cups warm orange juice mixed with 1/2 cup warm water
> 1/4 cup vegetable oil
> 1/2 cup pecans, chopped
> 1/2 cup dried apricots, chopped
> Cornmeal

In a large mixing bowl, combine 2 cups flour, yeast, sugar, cinnamon, salt and baking soda. Stir in orange juice, water and oil; beat on low speed until moistened. Beat on high speed for 3 minutes. Stir in pecans, apricots and remaining flour. The batter should be quite stiff. Grease two 8-inch x 4-inch x 2-inch pans. Dust with cornmeal. Pour batter in pans and cover. Let rise in a warm place until doubled, about 45 minutes. Preheat oven to 350 degrees and bake loaves for 35-40 minutes or until golden brown. Immediately remove bread from pans cool on wire racks.

Makes 2 medium loaves

PUMPERNICKEL BREAD

> 1 cup rye flour
> 1/2 cup each cornmeal and whole wheat flour
> 2 tsps. baking powder
> 1/2 tsp. baking soda
> 1/2 tsp. caraway seeds
> 2 eggs, beaten
> 1/4 cup molasses
> 3/4 cup milk
> 1/4 cup vegetable oil
> 1/2 Tbs. sesame seeds

Preheat oven to 350 degrees. Grease an 8-inch x 3-inch loaf pan. In a large bowl, mix together dry ingredients. In a small bowl, beat eggs, molasses, milk and oil and pour over dry ingredients, stirring to blend well. Pour batter into prepared pan. Sprinkle with sesame seeds. Bake about 50-60 minutes or until a cake tester inserted into center of bread tests clean. Remove bread from pan and cool on a wire rack.

Makes 1 loaf

BEST BANANA BREAD

About 7 years ago, I developed a concept called 'Juice Works.' It was a very special place that provided fresh juice and smoothies made to order. The business grew very quickly and before I knew it, lines formed outside and around the building everyday for lunch. Several of my regular customers asked for something that would go well with the drinks and that would provide a little more substance for lunch. I put the task to my mother who for months perfected her favorite banana bread recipe. "Perfected" was a understatement. The result was overwhelming for all of us. Over the next year a regular clientele developed that came exclusively for the banana bread. I am proud to share this recipe with you.

2 sticks Blue Bonnet margarine
1 1/4 cups sugar
3 eggs
4 cups flour
1 tsp. baking soda
4 tsps. baking powder
2 tsps. vanilla
6 large ripe bananas
1 tsp. baking soda

Preheat oven to 350. In a large bowl, beat margarine and sugar together, then add eggs one at a time and beat until creamy. Add 2 cups flour and baking powder. Add vanilla and bananas. Beat until smooth, then add the rest of the flour and the baking soda. Grease a large loaf pan and place down on the bottom a piece of tin foil that fits the bottom portion of the pan. Fit the entire interior of the pan with parchment paper and crease down in corners. Paper will stick because of the grease. Spray the paper with cooking spray. Bake 1 1/2 hours. Lower oven to 325 degrees for 30 minutes or until a toothpick tests clean when inserted in center.

Makes 1 large loaf

PANETTONE

This beautiful bread requires patience and love for perfect results. You will need a Panettone mold. If you do not have one use a lunch size paper bag.

> 1 packet active dry yeast
> 1/4 cup warm water
> 1/2 cup unbleached all-purpose flour
> 1/2 cup dried apricots, chopped
> 1/4 cup brandy
> 5 Tbs. softened butter
> 2 eggs + 4 yolks
> 3/4 cup sugar
> 1/4 cup warm water
> 1 Tbs. vanilla
> 5 cups unbleached all purpose flour + 1 Tbs. flour
> 1 Tbs. orange zest
> 1 Tbs. lemon zest

Butter a panettone mold or fold down top of bag to form a cuff so that the bag stands about 4-5 inches high. Butter inside of bag generously and place on a baking sheet.

To make the sponge:

In a medium mixing bowl dissolve the yeast in the warm water. Add the flour and stir with a spoon or your fingers to make a loose, almost liquid dough. Cover the bowl with plastic wrap and let rise in a warm place for at least 6 hours or overnight. In a small bowl combine apricots and brandy and let marinate for at least 4 hours.

In a large bowl, stir together the butter, eggs, yolks, sugar, warm water, and vanilla together. Drain the marinated apricots in a small strainer set over a bowl and press on the apricots with a spoon to extract the excess liquid. Set the apricots aside and add the liquid to the egg mixture. Add the sponge and mix well with your hands. Add the flour, about 2 cups at a time, mixing with your hands until a dough forms. Turn it out onto a floured work surface and knead for 5 to 10 minutes or until smooth and elastic, adding more flour as needed to keep from sticking. Butter a large bowl, place the dough inside and turn it to coat it with the flour. Cover with a clean cloth and let rise for 6 hours in a warm place.

Preheat oven to 400 degrees. Punch down dough and place on a floured surface. Flatten the dough with your hands and sprinkle with the lemon and orange zest. In a small bowl, mix the apricots with the 1 Tbs. flour and sprinkle the mixture over the dough. Fold the dough in half, press the edges together, and knead to distribute the fruit. Continue to knead for 5 to 10 minutes or until the dough is smooth, adding more flour if necessary. Place the dough in the mold, cover with a clean cloth, and let rise for 35 minutes in a warm place.

Cut an "X" in the top of the bread. Bake for 5 minutes, and reduce heat to 375 degrees and bake for 10 minutes. Reduce the heat to 350 degrees and bake for 30 to 35 minutes longer, or until a toothpick inserted in the center tests clean. If the top begins to brown too much, cover the bread loosely with a piece of tin foil. When finished, place the bread while still in the mold on a rack to cool for about 30 minutes. When cool, remove from mold.

Makes 1 large or 2 medium loaves

SICILIAN EASTER RING

    1 packet rapid rise yeast
    1/4 cup warm water
    2/3 cup warm milk
    2 Tbs. butter or margarine, room temperature
    1/3 cup sugar
    3/4 tsp. salt
    4 cups all-purpose flour
    1/2 tsp. cinnamon
    1/2 tsp. vanilla
    2 eggs
    2 Tbs. olive oil
    5 hard boiled eggs, colored red with food coloring
    1 egg yolk beaten with 1 tsp. water

Preheat oven to 350 degrees. In a large mixing bowl, dissolve yeast in warm water for 5 minutes, or until foamy. Stir in milk, butter, sugar and salt until butter melts. Blend in 2 cups flour. Using an electric mixer with a dough hook, beat until dough is elastic, about 5 minutes. Beat in cinnamon, vanilla and eggs. Add 1 1/2 cups more flour to make a soft dough. Knead the dough by hand on a floured surface until it is smooth and supple. Place in a large bowl and brush top lightly with olive oil. Cover with a clean towel and let rise in a warm place until doubled. Punch dough down and place on a floured surface. Divide the dough into 3 equal parts and roll each portion into a 24-inch strip. Place strips side by side on a large greased baking sheet and braid loosely. Curve the braid to form a circle and pinch the ends tightly to seal. Press the colored eggs pointed ends down at even intervals over the dough. Cover and let rise until the dough is well risen, about 35 minutes. Brush lightly with egg yolk and bake for 30 minutes or until bread is golden brown. Cool on a wire rack.

1 large ring

PISTACHIO CAKES

     1 cup pistachios, shelled
     1 cup sugar
     1/4 tsp. salt
     4 eggs, separated
     1 Tbs. orange zest
     2 drops green food coloring
     1/2 cup potato flour

Preheat oven to 325 degrees. Place pistachios in a food processor or blender with sugar and salt. Process to finely grind. Place in a large mixing bowl. In a small bowl, whisk egg whites until stiff and set aside. Add the egg yolks and zest to the nut mixture and gently fold in whites and food coloring. Mix in flour thoroughly. Lightly spray 3-inch cake pans or souffle molds. Pour batter into pans and bake for 20 minutes or until a toothpick tests clean. Remove from pans and cool on a wire rack.

Makes 10 cakes

RIBBONS

     2 cups all purpose flour
     3 eggs
     4 Tbs. butter, room temperature
     1/4 tsp. salt
     Vegetable oil for frying
     3/4 cup powdered sugar

Using an electric mixer, mix together flour, eggs, butter and salt. Cover the dough with a damp towel and let rest for 30 minutes. On a floured surface, roll dough out into a translucent, 1/4 inch thick sheet. Use a fluted ravioli wheel to cut the sheet into 1-inch strips. In a large skillet heat 3-4 inches of oil. When it is hot, deep fry the ribbon strips until puffed and golden. Remove with a large slotted spoon and let drain on paper towels. Using a sifter, sprinkle each ribbon with powdered sugar.

Makes 3 dozen

WINE

It is true that Italy has a drink for every occasion and a trip through the countryside, with its dotted landscape of vine-yards, proves to solidify that no where else in the world is wine enjoyed more. Years ago, the wine produced in Sicily was sweet and had a very high alcohol content, but today's Sicilian wines, particularly the Marsalas, have won international acclaim for their flavor and depth.

Wine making in Sicily dates back as early as the eighth century, B.C., when the Romans toasted their celebrations with a glass of wine. The Arab-Sicilian musicians sang praises to the grape, restoring the reputation of winemaking after the Norman occupation had halted production. Thank goodness!

CHEESE

Italians love all cheeses, hard or soft, fresh or aged. Cheese making is centuries old and continues today on many small Italian country farms. These world renowned cheeses have become household words to us all.

Here are some of the most popular:

Asiago is a firm and rich cow's milk cheese named after the region.

Fontina is similar to cow's milk Swiss cheese but without the holes!

Gorgonzola is a strong, ivory colored cow's milk blue cheese with blue green veins.

Mascarpone is from the Lombardy region. Its rich, cow's milk flavor is a cross between cream and soft sweet butter.

Mozzarella is soft and usually made from water buffalo or cow's milk. Mozzarella means 'twisted' or 'torn off,' so you will also find this cheese in braids. It is an excellent melting cheese.

Parmesan, a hard textured cheese, is most famous for grating on pasta. Best quality parmesan is imported from Reggiano and stenciled with the name on the rind.

Pecorino is used for both cooking, eating and grating, depending on its age. Sometimes it is referred to as Romano and substituted for Parmesan. It can be found plain or studded with black pepper corns.

Provolone is a rich cow's milk cheese that is excellent alongside fresh Mozzarella and a natural with classic dishes such as lasagne.

Ricotta is made from whey or milk and is a creamy curd cheese, resembling cottage cheese. Ricotta can be found in all courses from antipasto to dessert.

OLIVES

Olive trees are thick throughout the hills of Italy. Often the trees are harvested with sticks or by hand in some remote areas, then they are collected in nets and transported to a central area. They are mashed into a paste and pressed for oil or selected for consumption. The Kalamata is one of the most popular varietals and is often called the 'Greek' olive. It is a ripe, purple, black olive. Other Italy varieties include the large green Sicilian and tiny Calabrese green olives.

OLIVE OIL

A little olive oil history

Homer called it "liquid gold.' In an ancient Greek ritual, athletes rubbed it all over their bodies. Olive oil has been more than mere food to the people of the Mediterranean. It has been medicinal, magical, an endless source of fascination and the fountain of great wealth and power, according to many sources. The olive tree, symbol of abundance, glory and peace, gave its leafy branches to crown the victorious in both friendly games and bloody war, and the oil of its fruit has anointed the noblest of heads throughout history. Olive crowns and olive branches, emblems of benediction and purification, were ritually offered to deities and powerful figures. Some were even found in Tutankhamen's tomb.

The belief that olive oil gave strength, prolonged youth, and perhaps even immortality, was widespread. In ancient Egypt,

Greece, and Rome, it was infused with flowers and grasses to produce both medicines and cosmetics. A list was excavated in Mycenae enumerating the aromatics (fennel, sesame, celery, watercress, mint, sage, rose, and juniper, among others) added to olive oil in the preparation of ointments.

Italy and Spain are now the most prolific producers of olive oil, although Greece is still very active. There are about thirty varieties of olives growing in Italy today, and each yields particular oil with its own unique characteristics. The price of extra-virgin olive oil varies greatly. The two most influential factors are the region where the oil is produced and the harvesting methods employed. Certain locations yield more bountiful harvests. Consequently, their oil is sold for less. Olive trees planted near the sea can produce up to 20 times more fruit than those planted in hilly inland areas like Tuscany. It is in these land-locked areas that the olive trees' habitat is pushed to the extreme; if the conditions were just a little more severe, the trees would not survive.

HERBS

Italian climate allows for herb growing all year round. Local markets are never without the standard handful of basic herbs we in the States have come to know as Italian spices. Herbs are hearty and easy to grow, but if time and space are limited, it's easy to find them in most grocery and specialty stores. These few herbs are used in all Italian cooking and especially in our Sicilian kitchen.

BASIL is our favorite tomato and salad herb. There are several varieties to choose from. Look for young and tender bunches. Older basil tends to get very intense and bitter. When working with basil tear the leaves as you need them. When they are cut, the edges will often turn black.

BAY LEAVES give lots of depth to soup, stews and grilled meats. Both dry and fresh leaves are readily available.

MINT is primarily used with fruit, vegetables and as a pretty garnish for desserts.

OREGANO is used for many sauces.

PARSLEY is the universal herb. Italian flat-leafed parsley has a very vivid flavor and we use it freely in everything from salad dressings to pasta.

ROSEMARY, our favorite focaccia herb, grows both in desert areas and the seaside villages in Northern Italy. It is sometimes called 'sea dew' and has a sweet, pungent flavor.

THYME is intense and a little goes a long way. We use it sparingly with fish, meat, poultry and tomatoes.

CHAPTER 9

PIZZA-THICK & THIN, ROLLED AND FOLDED

The one thing for certain, is that to Sicilians, pizza is another form of bread.

Here are some known facts that give us an insight into the origin of pizza.

— Ancient Greeks ate flat, baked bread with assorted toppings called plankuntos. This flatbread may have been a derivative of something Babylonians ate in earlier centuries.

— The original Mozzarella cheese was made from the milk of Indian water buffalo in the 7th century. It was introduced to Italy in the 18th century.

— The world's first true pizzeria may have been 'Antica Pizzeria Port'Alba' which opened in 1830 and is still in business today at Via Port'Alba 18 in Napoli.

— Italian and Greek peasants ate earlier forms of pizza for several centuries before it became a hit among aristocracy. In 1889, a Neapolitan named Rafaele Esposito prepared pizza for King Umberto I and Queen Margherita, who apparently loved it.

— An Italian immigrant named Gennaro Lombardi opened the first U.S. pizzeria in 1895 in New York City.

— Pizza is now consumed all over the world, though travelers are often amazed by how different countries have adapted pizza to their own cultures.

— Pizza took the form that we are now familiar with in pre-Renaissance Naples, a large city in central Italy. Poor peasants used their limited ingredients like wheat flour, olive oil, lard, cheese and natural herbs to make seasoned, flat bread topped with cheese. Mozzarella cheese was one positive outcome from an Asian invasion that brought the water buffalo to Italy. Today the best Mozzarella cheese is still made from water buffalo milk.

THE FEARED AMERICAN TOMATO

Europeans returning from Peru and Mexico brought with them the tomato, which was originally thought to be lethally poisonous. Just how this myth came about is unclear, but as Southern Europeans overcame their suspicions, the tomato became enormously popular. Today, of course, the tomato is a crucial component of Mediterranean cuisine, and is still used in a majority of pizza recipes.

Before pizzerias became very popular, young male street vendors paraded Napoli with small tin stoves on their heads, calling out to attract pizza customers. This eventually led to the world's first pizzeria.

It's all in the crust!

BASIC PIZZA DOUGH

> 1 package active dry yeast
> 1 cup warm water
> 2 Tbs. sugar
> 1/2 tsp. salt
> 2 tsps. olive oil
> 2 3/4 cups all-purpose flour

In a large bowl, dissolve the yeast in warm water and sugar. Let stand 5 minutes or until foamy. Stir in salt, olive oil and add 2 cups flour. Using an electric mixer, beat the dough until it is elastic, about 5 minutes. Then stir in 3/4 cup flour to make a soft dough and knead until smooth and spongy, about 10 minutes. Place in a greased bowl, turning dough to grease top. Cover and let rise in a warm place for about 1 hour or until doubled in size.

Makes 2 medium pizza crusts

DEEP DISH SICILIAN DOUGH: THE SFINCIUNI

Unlike a thin pizza crust, this deep-dish pizza has a softer, thicker, bread-like texture that houses lots of filling. It is usually partially baked before the filling is added to ensure a completely cooked crust.

> 1 package active dry yeast
> 3/4 cup warm water
> 2 tsps. sugar
> 1/2 tsp. salt
> 3 Tbs. olive oil
> 2 cups unbleached all-purpose flour

In a large bowl, dissolve yeast in warm water and let stand 5 minutes or until foamy. Stir in sugar, salt and olive oil. Using an electric mixer, add 1 1/2 cups flour and beat 3-5 minutes. Stir in the rest of the flour to make soft dough, adding a little at a time. Turn dough out onto a floured surface and knead until smooth and elastic, about 10 minutes. Since dough will be quite sticky, it helps to moisten your hands with a little olive oil as you knead it. When dough is smooth and elastic, place it in a greased bowl, turning to coat top. Cover and let rise in a warm place until doubled in size or about 45 minutes.

CALZONE DOUGH

> 1 package active dry yeast
> 1 cup warm water
> 1/2 tsp. salt
> 2 tsp. olive oil
> About 3 cups all-purpose flour

In a large bowl, dissolve yeast in warm water and let stand for 5 minutes or until foamy. Stir in salt, olive oil and gradually incorporate flour a little at a time until a soft and slightly sticky dough forms. Turn out onto a well-floured surface and knead until smooth and no longer sticky, adding a little flour as needed to keep the dough from sticking. Place in a greased bowl, turning dough to grease top. Cover and let rise in a warm place for about 1 hour or until doubled in size.

ASSEMBLING PIZZA:

Grease two pizza pans. When the dough has risen, punch it down, knead it on a lightly floured surface, and shape into a smooth ball. Divide dough in half and roll out each half to a 1/2-inch thick disk. Gently pull each portion into an oval 12-14 inches long and about 8-10 inches wide. Place each oval of dough on prepared pizza pan. Continue to stretch the dough until the pan is completely covered. Brush dough generously with olive oil.

TRADITIONAL TOMATO SAUCE

Feel free to mix and match any of the toppings to suit your crowd, mood and season. Just have fun and come up with your own combinations. Use the best ingredients your budget will buy and remember that the sauce is a key element. Here's my family's traditional tomato sauce for pizza.

> 1 small onion, finely chopped
> 3 garlic cloves, minced
> 1 Tbs. olive oil
> 1 tsp. sugar
> 1/8 tsp. each salt and pepper
> 1/8 tsp. dried oregano
> 1/8 tsp. dried basil
> 1 12-oz. can tomato sauce

In a medium non-stick skillet, brown onion and garlic in oil over medium heat. Stir in sugar, salt and pepper. Crumble the oregano and basil with your fingers and add along with the tomato sauce. Stir and simmer for about 1/2 hour.

Makes sauce for 2 medium or 1 large pizza crusts.

SFINCIUNI di PALERMO

Before spreading sauce on pizza, try sprinkling sesame seeds on the dough. They are delightfully crunchy.

> 1 recipe sfinciuni dough, see Sicilian Dough, pg. 157
> 1 recipe tomato sauce, see recipe pg. 125
> Corn meal and oil for dusting pan
> 1 cup thinly sliced pepperoni
> 1 6-oz. can sliced mushrooms
> 2 cups Mozzarella cheese, shredded

Preheat oven to 375 degrees. Lightly oil a heavy 10-inch cast iron skillet or deep dish pizza pan. Dust with corn meal. Turn dough onto a lightly floured surface and knead briefly, gently deflating dough. Pat and stretch dough to cover bottom and about 1 1/2 inches up sides of prepared pan. The dough will shrink back at first. As you continue to stretch and press, it will conform to the pan. Bake for 20 minutes or until lightly browned, about 15 minutes. Remove from oven and spread sauce over crust, then evenly place pepperoni and mushrooms over the sauce and sprinkle with cheese. Bake until golden brown, about 15 minutes. Remove and serve immediately.

FOUR SEASONS PIZZA

This pizza is divided into four sections, representing the four seasons of the year.

    1 recipe basic pizza dough, see pg. 157
    1/4 cup olive oil
    1/2 lb. fresh mushrooms, thinly sliced
    1 small onion, finely chopped
    1 garlic clove, minced or pressed
    1 12-oz. can tomato sauce
    1 tsp. dried basil
    1/4 tsp. dried oregano
    2 Tbs. Parmesan cheese, grated
    Cornmeal
    4 marinated artichoke hearts, drained and quartered
    1 cup prosciutto, ham or salami, thinly sliced
    2 cups Mozzarella cheese, shredded

Heat 2 tablespoons olive oil in a non-stick skillet over medium heat and lightly brown mushrooms. Remove with a slotted spoon and set aside. Add onion to the pan and more olive oil as needed. Cook, stirring occasionally, until onion is soft, but not brown, about 5 minutes. Add garlic, tomato sauce, basil and oregano and cook, stirring occasionally, until thick, about 5 minutes. Remove from heat, stir in Parmesan and set aside.

Preheat oven to 450 degrees. When dough has risen, punch down and knead on a lightly floured surface. Shape into 1 or 2 smooth balls. Lightly spray 2 medium or 1 large pizza pan with oil and dust with corn meal. Roll out ball to 3/4-inch thickness and place in pans; stretch pizza dough to fit pans. Spread evenly with tomato sauce. Divide each pizza into 4 equal sections. Arrange mushrooms over 1/4 of each pizza. Place artichokes over the next section and brush them with the remaining olive oil. Cover the third section with prosciutto, and the last section with mozzarella. Bake on lowest oven rack for 15-20 minutes if making medium pizzas, or 25-30 for large. Pizza should be deep, golden brown. Serve immediately.

Makes 2 medium or 1 large pizza

GRILLED VEGETABLE PIZZA

> 1 recipe basic pizza dough, see pg. 157
> 1 small eggplant, thinly sliced
> 1 medium red onion, thinly sliced
> 2 roma tomatoes, peeled and chopped
> 1 zucchini, thinly sliced
> 2 green onions, chopped
> 1 Tbs. olive oil
> 1 garlic clove, chopped
> Cornmeal
> Pesto Sauce, see pg. 121

While pizza dough is rising, heat a barbeque grill. Marinate all vegetables briefly in olive oil and garlic. Grill until tender and set aside.

Preheat oven to 450 degrees. Lightly oil 2 medium or 1 large pizza pan and dust with cornmeal. When dough has risen, punch down, and lightly knead on a floured surface. Roll into 1 or 2 smooth balls. Roll dough and stretch to fit prepared pans. Arrange grilled vegetables on top of dough. Bake until crust is thoroughly golden brown, about 15 minutes. Remove and drizzle top of pizza with pesto and serve.

2 medium or 1 large pizzas

PIZZA MARGHERITA

In 1889, Rafaele Esposito of the Pizzeria di Pietro e Basta Cosi, now known as Pizzeria Brandi, baked a pizza in honor of the King Umberto I and Queen Margherita who had come to visit. In an effort to make the pizza a little more patriotic, he used red tomato sauce, white Mozzarella cheese and green basil leaves as toppings. Queen Margherita adored it and it has become synonymous with the word pizza. Pizzeria Brandi, now more than 200 years old, still proudly displays a royal thank-you note signed by Galli Camillo, 'head of the table of the royal household,' dated June 1889.

> 1 basic pizza dough, see pg. 157
> Cornmeal
> 6 oz. Mozzarella cheese, shredded
> 4 roma tomatoes, thinly sliced
> 1/4 tsp. salt
> 1/8 tsp. black pepper
> 1/4 cup fresh basil leaves, sliced into thin strips
> 1 Tbs. fresh oregano, chopped
> 2 Tbs. extra-virgin olive oil

Heat oven to 425 degrees. Lightly oil 2 medium or 1 large pizza pan and dust with cornmeal. When dough has risen, punch down, knead on a lightly floured surface and shape into 1 or 2 smooth balls. Roll out dough and stretch to fit into prepared pans. Place cheese on dough. Arrange the tomatoes on the cheese. Sprinkle pizza with remaining ingredients, using half of the basil and drizzling olive oil over the top. Bake for about 20 minutes or until crust is brown and cheese is melted. Sprinkle top with the remaining basil. Serve immediately.

Makes 2 medium or 1 large pizza

CALZONE THE PIZZA TURNOVER

Calzone are hearty pizzas that can be filled with whatever suits you. Here are two Sicilian standards.

1 recipe calzone dough, see pg. 158

Sausage filling:
3 mild or hot Italian sausage links
1 small onion, diced
1 garlic clove, minced
4 fresh mushrooms, sliced
1 green pepper, seeded and thinly sliced
1 small carrot, thinly sliced
1 8 oz. can tomato sauce
1 small can sliced black olives
1 tsp. dry basil
1/2 tsp. dried oregano
1/2 tsp. sugar
1/4 tsp. crushed red pepper flakes
2 cups Mozzarella cheese, shredded
1/4 cup Parmesan cheese, grated
1/4 tsp. each salt and pepper
Olive oil
Cornmeal

In a large non-stick skillet over medium heat, brown the sausage. Add onion, garlic, mushrooms, green pepper and carrot. Cook, stirring, until vegetables are limp, about 5-7 minutes. Stir in tomato sauce, olives, basil, oregano, sugar, and red pepper flakes. Reduce heat and simmer, uncovered for about 10 minutes. Set aside. When cool, fold in cheeses and season with salt and pepper.

To assemble calzone:

Heat oven to 425 degrees. Lightly oil a large baking sheet and dust with cornmeal. After dough has risen, punch it down and divide in half for 2 large turnovers, or in quarters for smaller ones. On a lightly floured surface, shape each piece into a ball. Roll dough balls into large 10-12 inch circles or smaller 8-inch circles for smaller turnovers. Brush surface of each circle with olive oil. Spread filling equally over half of each circle. Fold top half over filling, then press edges together. Roll 1/2-inch of pressed edges up and over. Seal and crimp. Transfer turnovers with a spatula to prepared sheets. Prick the tops of the calzone with a fork and lightly brush with oil. Bake until golden brown, about 15-20 minutes.

Makes 2 large or 4 medium calzone

Vegetable filling:

Following directions for previous filling, omitting the sausage. Cook vegetables in 2 to 3 tablespoons of olive oil and an additional 1/2 lb. of mushrooms. Add another teaspoon of oregano and additional 1/2 cup of Mozzarella. Increase the Parmesan to 1 cup.

STROMBOLI THE RECTANGLE PIZZA

1 recipe pizza or calzone dough, see pages 159-160
1/2 cup tomato sauce
1/4 tsp. each salt and pepper
1/2 tsp. each dried basil and oregano
1 cup Mozzarella cheese, shredded
2 oz. prosciutto or smoked ham, thinly sliced
20 large fresh basil leaves
1/4 lb. Genoa salami, thinly sliced
1 cup Provolone cheese, shredded

In a small skillet over medium heat, heat tomato sauce and seasonings for 5 minutes. Set aside.

Preheat oven to 400 degrees. Lightly oil a baking sheet. On a lightly floured surface, divide dough in half and press each into a 12-inch x 8-inch rectangle. Spread 1/2 cup Mozzarella over rectangles leaving a 1/2-inch border. Assemble 2 layers of sauce, ham, fresh basil leaves and salami on top of cheese. Starting with the long side, fold edge to center. Carefully fold again so folded side meets opposite edge. Pinch edge of dough into the fold to seal edges. Place on prepared sheet and bake for 20 minutes or until golden brown.

Makes 2 stromboli

FLATBREAD PIZZA

Mama May's great secret here is to mist the dough before all the topping is on to ensure a crisp crust.

> 1 packet rapid rise yeast
> 1 tsp. sugar
> 1 1/2 cups warm water
> 2 Tbs. olive oil
> 2-1/2 Tbs. Crisco
> 2-1/2 Tbs. nonfat dry milk
> 3-3/4 cups unbleached all-purpose flour
> 1-1/2 tsps. salt
> Cornmeal
> Olive oil and additional salt

In a large bowl, dissolve yeast and sugar in warm water and stir until foamy. Stir in oil, Crisco, and milk. Mix the flour and salt in a large bowl and make a well in the center. Pour the yeast mixture into the flour and stir until all the flour is incorporated. On a floured surface, knead dough, adding flour as needed to keep it from sticking, Dough will be soft and silky smooth in about 10 minutes. Place dough in an oiled bowl, turning dough to oil top. Cover and place in a warm area until dough has doubled, about 1 hour. While dough rises, make the topping. When dough is ready, lightly oil a large baking sheet and dust with cornmeal. On a lightly floured surface turn out dough and flatten firmly. Divide into thirds. Roll each piece into a ball and let rest, covered, for 15 minutes. Shape the balls into 6 round discs, 8-10 inches in diameter. Dimple tops with your fingers and brush with oil. Sprinkle lightly with salt. Cover dough with a towel and let rise again for about 1 hour. Heat oven to 425 degrees. Dimple dough again with your fingers, brush the discs with a little olive oil and sprinkle with salt. Mist the dough with a fine spray of water. Place in the oven and bake for 20 minutes or until lightly golden brown. While the crust is baking, prepare the topping.

Topping:

> 2 red onions, finely sliced
> 1 yellow pepper, finely sliced
> 1 red pepper, finely sliced
> 1 garlic clove, minced
> 2 Tbs. olive oil
> 1 Tbs. fresh basil leaves

In a large skillet, sauté all the ingredients, except basil, in oil over medium heat, until tender, about 15 minutes. Stir in the basil leaves. Spread topping onto baked dough discs. Bake for an additional 20 minutes or until lightly golden brown.

Makes 6 flatbreads

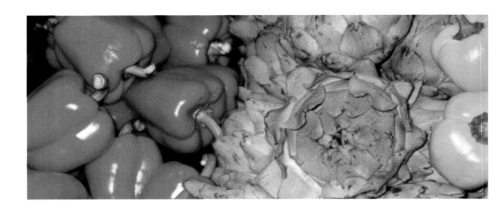

CHAPTER 10

VEGETABLES-ORDINARY TO EXTRAORDINARY

Sicilian food is not all spaghetti and meatballs! For centuries, peasants lived off the fruits of their field labor. Today the ground that was once a vision of disaster has become a symbol of peace and eternal life that produces fresh vegetables, herbs, fruits, olives and grapes.

How did it start? In the 9th century A.D., the Arabs arrived with troops and ordered peasants to forage for their food. The people returned with nuts, saffron from flowers, wild fennel and fish and the feasting began. The Arabs ruled for over 300 years and during that time brought sugar to Sicily, eventually replacing the honey. They also planted citrus orchards and gardens that even now are abundant with oranges and flowers. When the Spaniards finally conquered the Arabs, they brought with them the tomato and pepper. So many cultures brought foods, cooking styles and flavors to Sicily. We incorporated all of them into our rustic, practical kitchens and, as you'll see, eventually developed our own decidedly Italian way with vegetables.

EGGPLANT TOMATO DIP

2 Tbs. olive oil
1 medium eggplant, peeled and cut into 1/4-inch cubes
1/2 medium onion, chopped
1 14 oz. can stewed tomatoes
1/8 tsp. dried oregano
1/4 cup dry red wine
2 Tbs. red wine vinegar
2 Tbs. capers, drained
1/8 tsp. each salt and pepper
1 baguette, sliced 1/4-inch thick
Olive oil
Fresh thyme sprig

In a large skillet, heat olive oil over medium high. Sauté eggplant and onion. Cook, 10 minutes or until tender, stirring occasionally. Stir in tomatoes, oregano, red wine, vinegar, capers, salt and pepper. Bring to a boil. Reduce heat and simmer, uncovered, for 10 minutes or until liquid evaporated. Cool, cover and chill. Brush baguettes with olive oil and arrange slices in a single layer on an unheated broiler pan. Heat oven to broil and toast bread for 2-3 minutes, or until golden. Top the dip with the thyme and serve with the fresh croutons.

Serves 6

STUFFED ZUCCHINI

  2 large zucchini, each about 12-inches long,
      halved lengthwise
  2 Tbs. extra-virgin olive oil
  1/2 small medium onion, finely chopped
  2 tsps. all-purpose flour
  1/4 cup breadcrumbs
  1/2 tsp. dried basil
  1/8 tsp. black pepper
  1/2 cup milk
  1 egg, beaten
  1/3 cup Parmesan cheese

Heat oven to 350 degrees. Place zucchini cut side down in a large, square baking dish. Microwave on high for 2-3 minutes or until just tender. Scoop out pulp leaving a 1/4-inch border and set aside. Finely chop the pulp and reserve. In a medium saucepan, heat the oil and sauté the onion until tender but not browned. Add chopped zucchini and cook 1 minute more. Stir in flour, crumbs, basil and pepper. Add milk and cook until mixture is thick and bubbly. Then cook 1 more minute. Mix in egg and Parmesan. Remove from heat and spoon mixture into zucchini shells. Bake 25-30 minutes or until filling is lightly browned.

Serves 4

SAUTÉED SPINACH

> 3 Tbs. olive oil
> 1 garlic clove, minced
> 1 pkg. frozen spinach
> 1 tsp. garlic salt
> 1/8 tsp. black pepper

Heat the oil in a small skillet over medium. Sauté garlic, then add spinach, seasoning with garlic salt and pepper. Cover and simmer for about 10 minutes or until spinach is tender.

Serves 4

GREEN SALAD WITH CITRUS

> 1/2 grapefruit, peeled
> 1 blood orange, peeled
> 2 Tbs. red wine vinegar
> 3-4 Tbs. olive oil
> Salt and pepper to taste
> 1 tsp. onion or shallot, chopped
> 6 cups mixed salad greens

Place washed greens into a salad bowl. Over a small bowl, separate grapefruit and orange into segments. Squeeze the membranes to get all the juice. Mix the segments with the juice, vinegar, oil, salt and pepper. Add shallots, pour mixture over the greens and toss well.

Serves 4

EGGPLANT CUTLETS

If you place a heavy weight on top of the eggplant as it drains, the excess water will be removed even more quickly.

    3-4 small eggplants, about 2 pounds
    Salt
    1/8 tsp. black pepper
    2 cups Italian flavored breadcrumbs
    3 eggs, beaten
    3-4 Tbs. olive oil
    3 Tbs. Parmesan cheese
    3-4 fresh basil leaves

Cut eggplants lengthwise into thin slices; sprinkle each slice with salt and stack in a colander. Drain the eggplant at least 1 hour. Squeeze excess water from each slice. Place breadcrumbs in a shallow platter, season with salt and pepper. Place eggs in a shallow bowl. Dip the eggplant first into the eggs and then thoroughly coat with the crumbs. In a large non-stick skillet, heat the oil over medium heat. Fry the eggplant until golden brown on both sides. Drain on a paper-towel lined sheet. Serve hot, sprinkled with cheese and topped with basil.

Serves 4

SICILIAN COLESLAW

    1/2 small cabbage, thinly sliced
    2 Tbs. fresh Italian parsley, chopped
    1 carrot, grated
    1 Tbs. fresh dill, minced
    1 Tbs. sugar
    1/4 tsp. salt
    2 Tbs. olive oil
    2 tsps. red-wine vinegar, or to taste

In a small bowl, mix cabbage, parsley, carrot and dill. Sprinkle the mixture with sugar, salt and oil, tossing to combine well. Sprinkle the coleslaw with the vinegar, toss and serve.

Serves 2

STUFFED CABBAGE

    1 cup white or wild rice
    1 red cabbage, cut and leaves separated
    2 Tbs. butter
    1/2 cup Parmesan cheese, grated
    1/3 cup Romano cheese, grated
    1 egg, beaten
    1/4 cup fresh Italian parsley
    1/2 cup breadcrumbs
    1 Tbs. garlic salt
    1/8 tsp. black pepper
    2 10-oz. cans tomato soup

Heat oven to 350 degrees. Cook rice until just tender and set aside. Heat a large pot of salted water to boiling and cook cabbage until leaves are soft and pliable. Drain and set aside. In a large mixing bowl, mix together all ingredients except soup. Fill each cabbage leaf, and roll into packets. Place packets in a large, glass baking dish. Pour soup and 1 can of water over cabbage. Cover with aluminum foil and bake for 30 minutes. Baste and uncover during the last 5 minutes. Serve hot.

Serves 4

FENNEL AND OLIVE SALAD

> 1 medium fennel bulb
> 1/4 lb. fresh assorted herb-flavored olives, pitted
> 1 Tbs. Italian parsley, minced
> 3 Tbs. garlic-infused olive oil
> 1 Tbs. red wine vinegar
> 1 garlic clove, minced
> 1 tsp. dried oregano
> 1/8 tsp. black pepper

Remove the top of the fennel and cut the bulb into small chunks. In a small salad bowl, mix together fennel, olives and parsley. In another small bowl, whisk together remaining ingredients. Pour over salad. Chill and serve.

Serves 4

BAKED POTATO CASSEROLE

> 2 garlic cloves, minced
> 2 medium red onions, thinly sliced
> 2 Tbs. dried oregano
> 1/2 cup olive oil
> 2 lbs. medium baking potatoes, peeled and thinly sliced

1/2 cup water
2 Tbs. fresh basil, chopped

Preheat oven to 350 degrees. In a small bowl, mix garlic, onions, oregano, and olive oil. In a large, glass baking dish, make layers of potatoes, sprinkling herb mixture over each layer. Pour the water into the bottom of the baking dish, cover and bake for 30 minutes. Uncover the last 15 minutes and bake until light golden brown. Place fresh basil on top and serve hot.

Serves 4

RED PEPPER SAUTE

This is great over garlic toast or as part of an antipasto platter along with being a tasty side dish.

1 large red pepper, cut in thin strips
3 large green peppers, cut in thin strips
1 large yellow pepper, cut in thin strips
3 Tbs. olive oil
2 medium yellow onions, thinly sliced
1 bay leaf
1 garlic clove, minced
8 roma tomatoes, diced
1/2 tsp. salt
1/8 tsp. black pepper

In a large non-stick skillet, heat oil and sauté onion, bay leaf and garlic over medium heat until onion is translucent. Add peppers and cook until tender, about 10 minutes. Add tomatoes, salt and pepper and reduce heat to low. Simmer for 10 minutes and serve.

Serves 4

GARLIC MASHED POTATOES

Feel free to substitute roasted garlic for the fresh. It gives a very mellow flavor. Just omit the fresh and mix in the roasted garlic as the potatoes are mashed.

> 5 lbs. unpeeled russet potatoes, washed and scrubbed
> 5-7 garlic cloves, peeled and chopped
> 1 cup whipping cream, warmed
> 2 Tbs. butter, melted
> 1 tsp. each salt and white pepper
> 1 Tbs. parsley, minced

Place potatoes in a large pot with the garlic. Cover with salted water and heat to a boil. Cook until potatoes are fork tender, about 25 minutes. Drain in a colander. Place back in pot and whip the potatoes with the wire whisk attachment of an electric mixer. Add heated cream and butter and mix until smooth. Season with additional salt and pepper and serve sprinkled with parsley.

Serves 4-6

CARAMELIZED GARLIC VEGETABLES

Try this garlicky creation with your favorite fish and a platter
of wild rice.

> 1 small yellow onion, cut into thin strips
> 1/2 small red onion, cut into thin strips
> 2 Tbs. sugar
> 2 Tbs. extra-virgin olive oil
> 5 carrot sticks, cut in 1/8" thin strips
> 1 small zucchini, thinly sliced
> 1 small yellow squash, thinly sliced
> 6-8 mushrooms, thinly sliced
> Salt and pepper
> Pinch cayenne
> 8 garlic cloves, chopped
> 1/4 head broccoli flowerets
> Red wine vinegar

In a medium bowl, mix together onions and 1 tablespoon sugar.
In a large nonstick skillet, heat the olive oil over medium high
heat. Add the onions and carrots and sauté for two minutes.
Add the remaining vegetables, salt, pepper, cayenne and
remaining sugar to the skillet. Stir from time to time, for six
minutes, or until the onions turn a golden brown and begin to
caramelize. Add the garlic and broccoli and sprinkle with
vinegar. Cook two more minutes. Remove pan from heat.
Serve immediately.

Serves 4

GARLIC GREEN BEANS

1 1/2 cups water
1/4 tsp. salt
1 lb. fresh green beans, trimmed
1 large leek, cut into 1/4-inch slices
2 Tbs. butter
4 garlic cloves, finely chopped
1/2 tsp. fresh ginger, grated (optional)
1/2 tsp. coarsely ground pepper
1 Tbs. sesame seeds (optional)

In a large skillet, heat water and salt to boiling. Add beans and cook over medium heat, stirring occasionally, until the beans are crispy tender, about 10 to 15 minutes. Drain. Remove beans to a bowl. In the same skillet add the leeks and butter. Sauté the leeks until tender crisp, about 5 minutes. Add the beans and remaining ingredients except seeds and cook over medium heat until the garlic is tender, about 3 minutes. Serve topped with sesame seeds if desired.

CHAPTER 11

'DOLCI'- DESSERTS AND SWEETS

Desserts and sweets are part of the Sicilian heritage. In fact, Siciliy's love for all things sweet dates back to the 9th century when sugar was introduced to the island. Since then, desserts like our rich sweet breads, cookies, cakes, ice cream, cheese-cakes and cream puffs all found their way onto our tables.

Sicily is one of the world champions of edible marzipan, that colored, sweet, pliable mixture of almond paste and sugar. Fruits, animals, flowers and holiday shapes are all crafted from marzipan. How it started depends on who you talk to. Some think it began when a drought destroyed all crops but the almond, forcing villages to create almond bread, pie, soup, and ultimately, marzipan. After the famine passed, marzipan lived on and found its way to Lubeck Germany where the finest marzipan is still made today. Look for Lubecker Marzipan and you'll be in for a treat! Here are 2 ways to make your own.

Commercial bakeries grind almonds through granite rollers. At home, grind them as fine as you can in a food processor or blender. Soften Marzipan by adding small amounts of corn syrup. If it is too soft, add additional powdered sugar to it.

MARZIPAN

Uncooked Marzipan
1/4 lb. ground blanched almonds
1/4 lb. powdered sugar
1 egg white
1/4 tsp. salt

Cooked Marzipan
3 cups sugar
1 cup water
4 cups ground
    blanched almonds

To prepare the uncooked marzipan, knead together all of the ingredients until smooth. Store the marzipan in an airtight container or plastic bag overnight.

To make cooked marzipan, heat sugar and water in a medium saucepan and stir to dissolve sugar. Add nuts and cook until mixture does not stick to pan and forms a thick workable paste.

Remove from heat and place on a marble slab, wooden board or a cookie sheet. While marzipan is still warm, knead first with a wooden spatula and then by hand until smooth, about 5 minutes. Store in an airtight container or plastic bag.

DOLCE DICTIONARY

Biscotti literally means "twice baked." Cookies filled with nuts, fruit or chocolate are baked in a loaf, sliced and rebaked to make a dry hard cookie.

Cannoli are tubular shaped fried pastries filled with sweet cream or ricotta.

Cassata is a ricotta cream filled cake usually served on birthdays and weddings.

Crostate are any desserts using a pastry crust.

Cucciddati are thin cookies filled with figs.

Gelato is a very rich form of ice cream.

Granita is an Italian version of fruit ice.

Marzipan is a type of moldable paste made from almonds.

Panettone is a sweet yeast bread usually filled with nuts and fruit.

Panna Cotto is a type of custard, meaning "cooked cream," that is served with fruit.

Piñalotte are tiny fried pastry balls covered with honey and sprinkled with chocolate and candy.

Pizelle are wafer thin cookies flavored with anise.

Sfinci are a form of fried dough topped with honey

Spumoni is a triple flavored ice cream, often chocolate, strawberry and pistachio.

Tiramisu is a very rich dessert made with ladyfingers, mascarpone and espresso.

Zabaglione is custard dessert made with whipped egg yolks, Marsala and sugar.

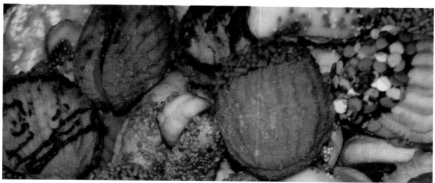

BISCOTTI DI MATRIMONIO

Use a firm sawing motion to cut straight down as you slice these cookies after the first baking.

    7 Tbs. cold unsalted butter
    1 cup sugar
    1 tsp. almond extract
    1 tsp. vanilla
    2 eggs
    3-1/2 cups flour
    1 tsp. baking powder
    1/2 tsp. baking soda
    1 cup slivered almonds
    2/3 cup dried currants

Preheat oven to 325 degrees. In a large mixing bowl, beat butter, sugar, almond extract, vanilla and eggs. Add flour, baking powder, and baking soda and mix together. Stir in almonds and currants. Fold together until nuts are evenly distributed in dough. Divide dough in half. Turn out onto a floured work surface and shape into 2 9-inch x 2 1/2-inch rectangles. Place on an ungreased cookie sheet, 3 inches apart. Bake for 25 minutes or until firm in the center. Let cool for about 5 minutes, then remove carefully using a spatula and transfer to a cutting board. Cut diagonally into 1/2- inch slices, Using your hands, carefully turn each cookie slice over once laying each piece on it's side; transfer to original baking sheet and return to the oven for another 10 minutes or until crisp and light golden brown. Remove biscotti and cool on a wire rack.

Makes 3 dozen

ANISE BISCOTTI

 2 cups sugar
 1 cup unsalted butter, room temperature
 4 eggs
 4 1/2 cups all-purpose flour
 4 tsps. baking powder
 1 tsp. salt
 1/4 cup brandy
 1/2 tsp. anise oil
 1 tsp. vanilla extract
 1 cup almonds, toasted and finely chopped

Preheat oven to 350 degrees. Line two heavy baking sheets with foil. In a large mixing bowl, beat sugar and butter until light and fluffy. Add eggs one at a time, beating well after each addition. Mix flour, baking powder and salt in a medium bowl. Combine brandy, anise oil and vanilla in a glass-measuring cup. Add dry ingredients and brandy mixture alternately to sugar mixture, beginning and ending with dry ingredients. Stir in almonds. Drop dough by spoonfuls onto prepared sheets, forming two 2-inch wide, 12-inch long strips on each sheet. Moisten fingertips and smooth dough into logs. Bake until golden and firm to touch, about 30 minutes. Transfer sheets to racks and cool logs completely. Reduce oven temperature to 300 degrees. Transfer cooled logs to work surface. Using a serrated knife, cut logs on diagonal into 3/4-inch thick slices. Arrange slices on ungreased baking sheets, laying each piece on it's side. Bake cookies until dry and slightly golden brown, or about 10 minutes on each side. Transfer to rack and cool.

Makes about 5 1/2 dozen

PISTACHIO BISCOTTI

2/3 cup sugar
1/4 cup butter, room temperature
1-1/2 Tbs. lemon juice
1 egg + 2 whites
1 tsp. vanilla
4 1/2 cups all-purpose flour
2 tsps. baking powder
1 cup shelled pistachios, chopped

Preheat oven to 350 degrees. In a large mixing bowl, beat sugar, butter, lemon juice, eggs and vanilla until fluffy. Gradually add flour and baking powder and mix until smooth. Fold in nuts. Divide dough in half. Shape into 2 10-inch x 3-inch rectangles, each 1/8-inch thick. Place on an ungreased cookie sheet. Bake for 25 minutes, or until center is firm. Cool on cookie sheet 15 minutes,then place on cutting board. Cut each rectangle cross-wise into 1/2-inch slices. Place slices, cut sides down, on cookie sheet and bake for another 10 minutes or until crisp and light golden brown. Immediately remove from cookie sheet to wire rack and cool.

Makes 2 dozen

CHOCOLATE DIPPED
CHERRY HAZELNUT BISCOTTI

3 cups sugar
1 cup unsalted butter, room temperature
1 Tbs. Amaretto
4 eggs
4 tsps. orange zest
2 tsps. baking powder
1 tsp. vanilla
1 tsp. salt
6 cups all purpose flour
2 1/2 cups hazelnuts, toasted and coarsely chopped
1 3/4 cups dried tart cherries

Position 1 oven rack in the center and 1 rack in top third of oven. Preheat oven to 325 degrees. In a large mixing bowl, beat sugar, butter and Amaretto using an electric hand mixer. Add eggs one at a time, mixing until just blended. Mix in zest, baking powder, vanilla and salt. Add 3 cups flour, hazelnuts and dried cherries, beating to mix well. Add remaining flour, 1 cup at a time, stirring until incorporated. Transfer dough to floured work surface. Divide into 4 equal pieces. Knead each piece until dough holds together well. Form each piece into 9-inch x 3-inch log. Place 2 logs on each of 2 large ungreased baking sheets, spacing about 3 inches apart. Logs will spread during baking. Bake, rotating baking sheets after 15 minutes. Bake until biscotti are golden and feel firm when tops are gently pressed, about another 15 minutes. Cool logs on baking sheets 15 minutes. Using a long wide spatula, transfer logs to cutting board. Cut warm logs with a serrated knife, crosswise into 1/2-inch slices. Arrange slices cut side down on 2 baking sheets. Bake biscotti 10 minutes. Turn biscotti over; bake until light golden. Transfer to racks and cool completely.

Chocolate Dipping Sauce:
    1/2 cup milk chocolate pieces
    1-1/4 cups semi-sweet chocolate pieces
    1 Tbs. Crisco

Stir both chocolates and Crisco in the top of a double boiler. Heat water in bottom of double boiler and place chocolate over water. Heat until chocolate is melted and smooth. Remove from heat and dip 1 cut side of each biscotti into chocolate to cover about 1/4 inch of the cookie. As you dip biscotti, gently shake off excess chocolate. Place them, chocolate side up, on baking sheets. Refrigerate until chocolate is firm, about 35 minutes.

Variations:
Substitute 1 2/3 cup white chocolate pieces and 1 Tbs. Butter Crisco or add 1 teaspoon lemon zest to the chocolate.

Makes 6 dozen

'CUCCIDDATI' FIG FILLED COOKIES

Pastry:
>4 cups all purpose flour
>1/2 cup sugar
>1 tsp. baking powder
>Pinch salt
>1/2 cup lard
>1 cup milk

Filling:
>1 lb. dried figs
>3/4 cup toasted almonds, chopped
>1/4 cup orange zest
>2 Tbs. ground cinnamon
>1/4 tsp. ground cloves
>4 Tbs. honey
>1/2 tsp. black pepper
>1/4 cup water
>Colored candy sprinkles

In a large bowl, mix together the flour, sugar, baking powder and salt. Cut in the lard with a pastry blender or two knives to form a coarse cornmealy texture. Add milk very gradually to form a stiff dough. Knead mixture together for a few minutes or until it feels like pie dough, then shape it into a ball and refrigerate for at least an hour. Meanwhile, make the filling. Soak figs in warm water for 10 minutes, drain and place in a food processor. Add all remaining ingredients and process to thoroughly blend.

Preheat oven to 350 degrees. Knead the dough again briefly and roll to 1/8-inch thick on a floured surface. Cut into 3-inch x 5-inch rectangles using a pastry wheel. Fill each rectangle with a generous tablespoon of filling. Fold in half and moisten the edges with water. Press edges together. Using a small knife cut a series of slits along the sealed edge. Curve the cookie into a "C" crescent and "O" circle so that the cut edges fan out and show some of the dark filling. Place on a greased cookie sheet and bake for about 20 minutes. Cool. Make a thin icing with water and powdered sugar, lightly ice each cookie, then top with a few colored candy sprinkles.

Makes 2 dozen

ITALIAN MACAROONS

> 5 egg whites
> 1/2 cup granulated sugar
> 3 cups shredded coconut
> 3/4 lb. almonds, toasted and chopped
> 1 tsp. Amaretto liqueur
> 18 Maraschino cherries, halved or 3 dozen whole almonds

Preheat oven to 375 degrees. Lightly grease a cookie sheet. Using an electric mixer, whip the egg whites slowly, adding sugar until stiff peaks form. In a large mixing bowl, mix coconut, almonds, and Amaretto. Gently fold egg whites into nut mixture until all ingredients are thoroughly blended into a soft dough. Drop by tablespoonfuls onto prepared sheet. Top each cookie with a cherry half or whole almond. Bake for 10 minutes or until a light golden brown. Remove from oven and cool on a rack.

Makes about 3 dozen cookies

RASPBERRY ORANGE VENETIAN BARS

5 Tbs. plus 1 1/2 tsp. butter, room temperature,
4 Tbs. powdered sugar
3 Tbs. orange juice
1 tsp. vanilla extract
1-1/2 cups all-purpose flour
1 cup hazelnuts, finely chopped
1/2 cup raspberry jam
1 Tbs. orange zest

Cut butter into small pieces. In a large bowl, blend together butter, powdered sugar, orange juice and vanilla using an electric mixer. Gradually beat in flour and half of the hazelnuts. Mix together until dough forms. Shape dough mixture into a ball, wrap in wax paper and chill for 1 hour.

Preheat oven to 375 degrees. Grease a large baking sheet and roll the dough into a 1/8-inch thick rectangle. Pierce the rectangle with a fork. Bake for about 5-6 minutes. Meanwhile, melt the remaining butter in a small saucepan and stir in remaining nuts. Cook for 2-3 minutes or until nuts are light brown. Remove from heat and set aside. Blend together the raspberry jam and the orange zest and spread over the pastry shell. Spoon the nut mixture over the jam. Reduce oven to 350 degrees and bake for an additional 7-8 minutes or until golden brown. Carefully remove to a cooling rack. Slice into 3-inch bars.

Makes 1 dozen bars

TIRAMISU

Cake:
6 eggs, separated
2/3 cup powdered sugar
1 tsp. vanilla
2/3 cup cake flour

Filling:
1-3/4 cups whipping cream
1-3/4 cups powdered sugar
2-1/2 Tbs. Marsala wine
1/2 tsp. vanilla extract
2 cups Mascarpone cheese

Coffee syrup:
1 cup brewed espresso or strong coffee,
    room temperature
2 tsps. granulated sugar

Toppings:
8 ozs. bittersweet chocolate
8 whole strawberries

For Cake:
Preheat oven to 375 degrees. Coat a 13"x 9" baking pan with
vegetable oil spray and lightly dust with flour. Beat egg yolks
with an electric mixer until thick and light; then set aside. In
large bowl of electric mixer, beat egg whites and powdered
sugar with until still peaks form; gradually fold in egg yolks and
vanilla. Gradually fold in cake flour and fold until well blended.
Pour and spread batter evenly in prepared baking pan. Bake
10-12 minutes or until wooden pick inserted into cake tests
clean. Remove from oven and let cool 10 minutes. Then,
gently loosen cake edges with a metal spatula and invert onto
rack to cool completely.

For Filling:
In a large bowl of an electric mixer, beat whipping cream, powdered sugar, Marsala and vanilla until soft peaks form. Gradually add the Mascarpone cheese to the mixture and continue to beat at low speed until whipped cream mixture has texture and is stiff. Cover and refrigerate 30 minutes or until chilled.

To assemble tiramisu:
Mix together the coffee and sugar. With a serrated knife, cut cake into two equal layers, then place one layer on the bottom of an 8 or 9-inch glass baking dish. Spoon 1/2 cup of coffee over cake. Spread with half of filling, then top with second layer.
Repeat with remaining coffee and cream filling. After smoothing top layer, shave chocolate over the top of the Tiramisu. Refrigerate until serving time. To serve, cut into squares and serve topped with a berry.

Serves 8

ZUPPA INGLESE CAKE

This custardy cake is similar to the English Trifle.

Cake:
3/4 cup plus 1 Tbs. cake flour
Pinch of salt
3 eggs, separated
3/4 cup sugar

Filling:
3/4 cup diced mixed dried fruits
1 tsp. rum
1 cup milk

4 egg yolks
1/4 cup sugar
2 Tbs. all-purpose flour
1 tsp. butter
1 Tbs. lemon zest
1 Tbs. vanilla extract

Rum Syrup:
1/4 cup sugar
1/4 cup water
1 Tbs. rum

To assemble the cake:
1 1/2 cups heavy cream
2 Tbs. powdered sugar
Ground cinnamon
3-4 pieces diced dried fruit

For Cake:
Heat oven to 350 degrees. Lightly butter a 9-inch round cake pan. Line bottom with waxed paper. Butter paper and dust pan with flour. In a medium bowl, mix flour and salt; set aside. In a large bowl of an electric mixer, beat egg yolks at medium speed until lemon colored. Add sugar gradually and beat until mixture is thick and fluffy. Using clean beaters, beat egg whites until stiff, but not dry, until peaks form. Fold egg whites into yolks. Gradually fold in flour and pour into prepared cake pan. Bake for 25 minutes or until lightly browned and wooden pick inserted in center tests clean. Remove cake from pan and transfer to wire rack to cook.

Prepare Filling:
In a medium bowl, soak fruit and rum in 1 cup boiling water.
Let stand 15 minutes, or until fruit softens. In a small
saucepan, heat milk just to a simmer. Remove and let cool
until it is just warm. Whisk yolks and sugar in top of double
boiler. Gradually whisk in flour, then add milk. Place top of
double boiler over simmering, not boiling, water and whisk
constantly until mixture coats back of spoon, about 15 to 20
minutes. Remove to bowl of ice water. Stir in butter, zest,
vanilla, and dried fruits. Cool, stirring occasionally. Press a
piece of buttered waxed paper on top and refrigerate several
hours or overnight.

Prepare Syrup:
In a small saucepan, heat sugar and water to a simmer. Cook
until thickened and mixture coats back of spoon, about 8 minutes. Add rum and simmer 1 more minute. Remove from heat.

To assemble the zuppa:

Split cake in half horizontally with a serrated knife. Place one
layer on a serving plate. Sprinkle with rum syrup. Spread filling
over layer. Top with second layer. Cake can be loosely covered
at this point and refrigerated overnight. Whisk together cream
and powdered sugar until stiff peaks form. Spread cream over
cake. Sprinkle with cinnamon and top with dried fruit.

Serves 8

SICILIAN CASSATA CAKE

The Cassata cake is the most spectacular Sicilian specialty and dates back some 500 years. Named after an Arabic cake mold called a 'qas'ah,' this classic dessert is filled with a sweetened ricotta filling. The Arabs are also credited with inventing the almond paste that is used in the cassata, which is sometimes used in place of the traditional pistachio paste.

Additional credit for the invention of this fine cake must be given to the baker who fulfilled the wealthy man's request for a rich cake with a sweet topping, lots of rum liqueur, and pistachios.

Cake:
1/2 cup butter, room temperature
1 cup sugar
1/2 cup milk
3 egg yolks, beaten
1 tsp. vanilla
1 1/2 Tbs. lemon zest
2 cups cake flour
1/4 tsp. cream of tartar
1/4 tsp. salt

Filling:
1 15-oz. container Ricotta cheese
2 Tbs. half-and-half
1/4 cup powdered sugar
1/4 cup shredded coconut
3 Tbs. Amaretto

Frosting:
1 1/2 cups semisweet chocolate chips
3/4 cup brewed espresso or strong coffee
1/2 lb. chilled butter, cut into thin slices

Prepare Cake:
Preheat oven to 350 degrees. Coat a 9-inch x 5-inch loaf pan with vegetable oil spray and dust with flour. In a large bowl, using an electric mixer, beat butter and sugar. Mix in milk, egg yolks, vanilla and lemon zest until creamy. Gradually beat in cake flour, cream of tartar and salt. Pour and spread evenly into prepared loaf pan. Bake 50 minutes, or until wooden pick inserted into center tests clean. Cool 20 minutes; then invert onto rack to cool.

Prepare Filling:
In a large mixing bowl, beat together ricotta cheese, half and half, powdered sugar, coconut, and Amaretto until smooth.

To Assemble Cassata:

Using a serrated knife, slice the top, bottom and the two end crusts off cooled cake. Cut the cake horizontally into three even layers. Place bottom layer, cut side up, on large plate. Spoon one half of ricotta filling onto cake. Carefully place next layer of cake on top, making certain sides and edges are even. Spread with more ricotta; repeat with next layer and filling. Finish with a plain slice of cake on top. Gently press the layers together making them slightly compact. Cover loosely with waxed paper and refrigerate at least 4 hours to 'ripen.'

To Prepare Frosting:
Melt semisweet chocolate chips with espresso or black coffee in a small saucepan over low heat, stirring constantly until chocolate dissolves. Remove pan from heat and pour into bowl of an electric mixer. When cool, beat in 1/2 lb. butter, one piece at a time. Continue beating until mixture is smooth. Refrigerate frosting until it thickens to spreading consistency. When spreadable, assemble and refrigerate until serving time.

Serves 12

'CASSATEDDI'   SWEET CHICKPEA TURNOVERS

These pastries, like countless others, were originally made by the convent nuns and had to be specially ordered.

Pastry:
3-1/2 cups all-purpose flour
1/2 cup sugar
Pinch of salt
1/2 cup white wine
1/2 cup lard

Filling:
2 cups chickpeas, cooked and pureéd without salt
1/4 cup honey
1/4 cup sugar
1/4 cup pine nuts, toasted and chopped
1/4 cup almonds, toasted and chopped
1 tsp. ground cinnamon
1/4 cup semisweet chocolate bits
1/4 cup candied citron

Vegetable oil for frying
Ground Cinnamon
Super-fine sugar

For pastry:

In a large mixing bowl, blend together the flour, sugar and salt. Make a well and add wine slowly. Cut in the lard using a pastry blender or two knives. Knead dough for at least 15 minutes or until it is very smooth and elastic. Cover and let stand for one hour.

Preparing Filling:

In a large bowl, blend all ingredients well.

To assemble the cassateddi:

Roll out the dough to a very thin sheet, and cut into 3-inch circles, 1/4" thick. On each circle place a tablespoon of the filling. Fold the circle over into a half-moon shape, lightly moisten the edges with water, and pinch the edges to seal tightly. Heat about 3-inches of oil in a medium saucepan until very hot but not smoking. Fry turnovers until golden, lowering heat as needed to medium high if oil begins to smoke. Drain on paper towels and sprinkle with cinnamon and sugar.

Makes 3 dozen

FRESH FRUIT TART

Pastry:
2 cups all-purpose flour
1 cup granulated sugar
1/2 cup butter or margarine, softened
1 tsp. vanilla
3 eggs
1 tsp. lemon zest
1 tsp. fresh lemon juice
1/2 tsp. anise seed

Filling:

> 1/4 cup raspberry jam
> 1-1/2 pints fresh raspberries or blueberries, or a combination of both
> 2 kiwis, thinly sliced
> 1 Tbs. honey
> 1 8-oz.can Mandarin oranges, drained for garnish
> Whipped Cream

Preparing Pastry:

In a medium bowl, mix together all pastry ingredients to form a soft dough. Place it on a lightly floured surface and knead for 3-4 minutes or until dough holds together and is pliable. Shape into a ball, cover with plastic wrap and refrigerate for about 30 minutes or until firm. Heat oven to 350 degrees. Butter and flour a 10-inch tart pan with removable bottom or spring form pan. Pat dough evenly into pan, and prick the sides with a fork. Bake for about 30 minutes or until a wooden pick inserted in the center tests clean. Remove to a rack and cool completely.

Assembly:

Carefully remove pastry from pan. Spoon the jam onto the bottom of the tart. Starting with the raspberries or blueberries, place a circle of berries in the center, then create two circles of kiwis. Fill in the outside spaces with remaining berries. Drizzle honey over berries and kiwi; then garnish with mandarin orange slices. Serve with whipped cream.

Serves 8

GERLOMA'S CLASSIC CHEESE CAKE

Mama May always puts a wet towel in the sheet pan before baking to ensure an even texture.

2 8-oz. packages cream cheese, room temperature
8 ozs. sour cream
1/2 cup sugar
2 eggs
1 Tbs. vanilla
1/2 cup heavy cream
2 cups graham cracker crumbs
2 Tbs. butter, softened
2 Tbs. sugar

Preheat oven to 325 degrees. In a large bowl of an electric mixer, blend cream cheese, sour cream and sugar. Beat until smooth. Gradually add eggs, one at a time, vanilla and cream. Beat until smooth and set aside. In a medium mixing bowl, mix together crumbs, butter and sugar and press firmly into a 9 or 10-inch spring form pan. Pour in cream cheese mixture. Place cloth towels on the bottom of a cookie sheet and place cake pan on towels. Pour about 2 cups water over the cloth towels until towels are completely moistened. Bake cheesecake for 50-55 minutes or until a wooden pick place in the center tests clean.

Serves 10

INDEX